DESIGN YOUR OWN EFFECTIVE EMPLOYEE HANDBOOK

W0010415

How to Make the Most of Your Staff—With Companion CD-ROM

Michelle Devon

Design Your Own Effective Employee Handbook: How to Make the Most of Your Staff—With Companion CD-ROM

ISBN-13: 978-0-910627-79-5   ISBN-10: 0-910627-79-7

Library of Congress Cataloging-in-Publication Data

Devon, Michelle, 1971-
  Design your own effective employee handbook : how to make the most of your staff with companion CD-ROM / by Michelle Devon.
     p. cm.
  Includes bibliographical references and index.
  ISBN-13: 978-0-910627-79-5 (alk. paper)
  ISBN-10: 0-910627-79-7 (alk. paper)
  1. Employee handbooks--United States. I. Title.

  HF5549.5.E423D48 2007
  658.4'55--dc22
                    2007002040

EDITOR: Marie Lujanac • mlujanac817@yahoo.com
PROOFREADER: Angela C. Adams • angela.c.adams@hotmail.com
ART DIRECTION: Meg Buchner • megadesn@mchsi.com

Printed in the United States

We recently lost our beloved pet "Bear," who was not only our best and dearest friend but also the "Vice President of Sunshine" here at Atlantic Publishing. He did not receive a salary but worked tirelessly 24 hours a day to please his parents. Bear was a rescue dog that turned around and showered myself, my wife Sherri, his grandparents Jean, Bob and Nancy and every person and animal he met (maybe not rabbits) with friendship and love. He made a lot of people smile every day.

We wanted you to know that a portion of the profits of this book will be donated to The Humane Society of the United States.

–Douglas & Sherri Brown

THE HUMANE SOCIETY
OF THE UNITED STATES ©

The human-animal bond is as old as human history. We cherish our animal companions for their unconditional affection and acceptance. We feel a thrill when we glimpse wild creatures in their natural habitat or in our own backyard.

Unfortunately, the human-animal bond has at times been weakened. Humans have exploited some animal species to the point of extinction.

The Humane Society of the United States makes a difference in the lives of animals here at home and worldwide. The HSUS is dedicated to creating a world where our relationship with animals is guided by compassion. We seek a truly humane society in which animals are respected for their intrinsic value, and where the human-animal bond is strong.

Want to help animals? We have plenty of suggestions. Adopt a pet from a local shelter, join The Humane Society and be a part of our work to help companion animals and wildlife. You will be funding our educational, legislative, investigative and outreach projects in the U.S. and across the globe.

Or perhaps you'd like to make a memorial donation in honor of a pet, friend or relative? You can through our Kindred Spirits program. And if you'd like to contribute in a more structured way, our Planned Giving Office has suggestions about estate planning, annuities, and even gifts of stock that avoid capital gains taxes.

Maybe you have land that you would like to preserve as a lasting habitat for wildlife. Our Wildlife Land Trust can help you. Perhaps the land you want to share is a backyard—that's enough. Our Urban Wildlife Sanctuary Program will show you how to create a habitat for your wild neighbors.

So you see, it's easy to help animals. And The HSUS is here to help.

The Humane Society of the United States
2100 L Street NW
Washington, DC 20037
202-452-1100
www.hsus.org

CONTENTS

FOREWORD

A s a professional human resources consultant with experience in a variety of industries and organizations large and small, I've never met a manager who wasn't surprised at the amount of time spent on "people issues."

Of course, time spent rewarding and recognizing employees for terrific performance is the fun part, and no one complains about that, but the time managers spend dealing with "negative" employee relations issues is much greater, and it is an unbelievable drain! A drain of energy, resources, and *time* that could be spent on a company's core mission. *And it is avoidable.* The simple truth is that a solid employee handbook helps prevent negative employee issues and helps to create healthy workplaces.

Over relatively short periods of time managers in even the smallest of companies are peppered with hundreds—no, thousands—of questions from employees regarding workplace policies and procedures. Consistency in handling employee inquiries and practicing non-discrimination are a requirement in today's business environment and can literally mean the difference between success and failure for a small business. Spelling out human resources guidelines in a simple, user-friendly employee handbook is an extremely effective leadership tool that ensures consistency and fairness and frees your resources to focus on what matters most for your company.

So why *don't* organizations reduce their human resources policies to writing? Why *not* create your own employee handbook? The most common barriers I've witnessed include misconceptions regarding time and expertise. Folks just don't believe they have the resources or skills required to dedicate to such a large and complicated project. With this handbook, these barriers (and more!) are immediately overcome. This comprehensive handbook not only provides all of the necessary templates, forms, suggestions, and resources needed to create a handbook, it also walks the lay user through the process, step by simple step. Now *anyone* can create a top quality employee handbook using a sound, collaborative process that will stand the test of time and help create the kind of workplace where employees can *thrive*. In today's tight labor market and competitive global economy, *it just makes sense*.

Rose Amberson, MSW, SPHR
President, Capital HR Services, Inc.
Pembroke Pines, Florida
954-665-7673
rgemsw@aol.com

Capital HR Services, Inc., provides capital human resource solutions to organizations large and small, including talent, training, and human resource compliance programs. Ms. Amberson is a former Vice President of Human Resources for Boca Raton, Florida, Community Hospital where she successfully developed and implemented a strategic human resources plan for the more than 2,300 employees. She is also a former Vice President in charge of training and development at Seitlin Human Resources of Miami and Fort Lauderdale, Florida.

PREFACE

An employee handbook is an indispensable workplace tool, because it can help your company communicate with employees, govern its workers and managers, streamline its organization, and protect itself from lawsuits. If you have decided it is a good time to start writing your employee handbook, you have made the right decision to purchase this book! It takes you through the process of developing, writing, updating, and distributing an employee handbook. From the first welcome page all the way to sample forms, you will be walked through the entire process, step by step with information and resources to aid you along the way. Whether you are writing an employee handbook for the first time from page one or are updating and adding to an existing handbook, be confident that you will find help here.

Whether you are hiring your own employees or you are involved in a human resources endeavor with many departments, your company can benefit from a well-written and properly formatted employee handbook. Simply put, an employee handbook is the company's way of communicating information and policies to employees in a format that the employee may refer to when needed to meet the conditions and terms of employment, while being informed of the benefits available to them.

Employees are not mind readers. Although you may know what the company's practices and policies are, other employees, managers, and supervisors have no place to turn for this information, creating an environment ripe for trouble, both legal and practical. Providing your employees with a handbook that spells out your company's benefits, policies, and procedures makes great sense, practically and legally. Every employee receives the same information about the rules of the workplace; your employees will know what you expect from them (and what they can expect from you); and you will buy yourself valuable legal protection if an employee challenges you in court. You cannot write an employee handbook that will cover every possible workplace situation. It is best to make this clear to your employees by saying so in the handbook; otherwise, your employees may argue that any action you take outside of that explicitly set forth in the handbook is unfair.

At some point, nearly everyone who has ever been employed has been issued some form of an employee handbook. From positions in fast food restaurants, mechanic shops, and industrial trades to administrative services and white-collar management positions, most employees receive something like a handbook. It sums up the company, its mission and vision, human resources guidelines, benefits, and regulations for the company and the employee. Your company, no matter how large or small, can benefit from having an employee handbook.

A well written handbook can provide training and protection for everyone in your company. It may be the only training tool some businesses will ever need. It can cut training and orientation costs down and it can help with legal matters. It can shield you when you need to be protected legally by providing a written document, especially when you have an employee's signature indicating receipt of a copy of the handbook. When the power of written proof is needed, you will be glad you have an active handbook in force for your business.

One word of caution here: while we encourage you to have legal counsel review your finished handbook, we advise that you check beforehand because in many states, any handbook is regarded as an employment contract. Loose wording such as "We will be fair to our employees" can easily be used against the company. Because employers are responsible for preparing the handbook, courts usually interpret any vague provisions in favor of employees if they sue. In addition, listed disciplinary procedures, if not followed to the letter, can be used to contest a firing.

However, in favor of the written handbook, courts generally view both written and verbal policies as a contract. Verbal policies can be implied or given by someone with no authority to make promises, while a written document is the company's best chance of not having a court case become the owner's word against that of the employee. From the standpoint of the firm's bottom line, therefore, a compelling reason to have a good handbook is to prevent or settle disagreements and avoid legal disputes, particularly in the areas of firing and discipline.

When your company is ready to hire employees, the first step in this process should be to determine certain rules regarding conditions and environment of the workplace. Establishing clear rules up front on issues such as work hours, smoking policies, benefits, leave time, and other basic company regulations can be critical. It is important to obey local, state, and national labor and anti-discrimination laws as well as the regulations put in place to implement those laws. All are critical to protect the company and the employee, as well as providing a means to implement workplace conditions and rules in a fair manner to all employees.

It is important to have some type of written documentation that spells out all the important aspects for both the company and the employee, something that both parties can refer to in times of dispute as well as setting a standard to be followed that is equal for everyone. That is what an employee handbook is: a guide for employees for quick reference about the most common workplace rules, as well as access to information about the company—compiled in one convenient well-written handbook and applied justly.

Even if your company has already established rules and regulations in an employee handbook, this guide will help you review those regulations. Maybe you need to establish some standards that may be missing while making sure the current ones are accurate. You can then format them in one organized document to distribute to the staff.

What better way to lower stress for employees? It can only be to the company leaders' advantage to see that employee relations run smoothly. Smart supervisors have discovered the easiest way to do this is by creating an ideal employee handbook.

"Time is money" cuts deepest when managers and supervisors are staring into the face of adversity. When their troubles are the result of poor employee relations, they would agree that a handbook would have saved time and guided them to a solution. Handling communication problems after the fact can be difficult and time consuming.

This book can save employers time and money. It can solve problems for supervisors when they need back-up to support an insubordination ruling. It is the final word or the governing law of the company. Frankly, if the company does not have one, it deserves to waste time dealing with repetitive questions and petty problems. When the important issues are in writing, you have legal legs to stand on, and you can stand firm.

A boss relies on managers to provide good working conditions. Managers are supposed to handle difficult employee relations while maintaining schedules, meeting production, and keeping costs in check. If employee relations are not up to par, sub-standard production is inevitable, and the company CEO or owner will look first to middle management if the company shows signs of losses. Workers who are deprived of dignity, humiliated, or treated in ways that are just plain mean are more likely to look for some revenge through the legal system—and juries are more likely to sympathize with them. For example, if you march fired workers off the premises under armed guard, publicize an employee's personal problems, or shame a worker in public for poor performance, you can expect trouble.

The process of creating a handbook will force your company's management to think about every aspect of its relationship with employees. Rather than doing things just because that's the way they've always been done, you can reflect on how employees have been treated and consider whether any changes are in order. Writing your own company policy and employee handbook is just plain smart. It is good business practice and it is great for saving time spent on the little things that can turn into gigantic time gobblers.

Shall we get busy learning how to develop your own company employee handbook? Best of all, we will keep it simple.

INTRODUCTION

Employees can make or break a business. Employee relations have to be good in any company for the company to thrive. One of the best ways to ensure good employee relations is through effective communication often through the written word.

There are four main reasons a company or small business needs an employee manual. The first is obvious: legal protection from potential lawsuits. The second is the time factor. If a company has an employee handbook, management will spend less time answering questions and more time invested in production. The third reason is to be fair in handling employee problems and complaints. If there is a manual to follow that details how the company reacts to employee situations, everyone gets a fair shake! Finally, it can be a back-up or "plan B" when there is nowhere left for a manager or an employee to turn. If it is in the "book," there is no reason to doubt its authenticity. It is the law-handed-down.

The spoken word is remembered for a short time. As the written word, the information is confirmed or set in stone. It cannot be challenged as effectively as spoken rules and requests. You may have experienced times when you, as the company owner or manager, had to move quickly to meet your company's expectations without an opportunity to deal with employee opposition. If you have a handbook in place, you will face fewer challenges in interpretation of your actions.

An employee handbook can have one sole purpose—to explain the employer's goals, expectations, rules, and what the employee can expect from his or her relationship with the company. It helps leaders in the company direct their teams more effectively. Supervisors can manage with greater success, and the company is protected from frivolous lawsuits. It allows the employee to view their rights and allows the company to explain their goals to the workforce, detailing how they handle certain situations. It provides answers to difficult questions and is used as a guideline for day-to-day actions.

An employee handbook sets forth the company's vision. New employees have no way of knowing the company's goals. They do not know the mission statement and they have no way of knowing the company's expectations of them. Even if they are told in an initial orientation, five years down the road they may have a question about a certain policy and they expect an answer.

Just a word here about the term "orientation." Perhaps in your company, the term "probationary period" is more common than "orientation." We recommend that you accustom yourself and others to avoid the term "probationary periods of employment." Otherwise, the handbook may imply that employees are entitled to continued employment after the probation is over. Instead use terms such as "training," "orientation," or "trial" period. This caution would apply to disciplinary periods as well.

The handbook presents policies and promotes fairness. Employees like consistency within a company, and an employee handbook allows a company to be consistent in their employee relations. An employee who feels unfairly treated is a bad situation just waiting to erupt.

DESIGN AND LEAD

The employee handbook allows you to communicate, effectively giving you a voice in dealing with your employees in a fair and impartial tone. You can write the handbook for your company in any format you want, but ideally it will be in a professional, friendly manner. Just remember, if you are the boss, the handbook is an extension of you—your views, policies, ideas, and goals for the company.

While there are obvious benefits to protecting yourself and your company legally by having a handbook, most small business owners view their staff not as adversaries but rather as members of the same team, working toward shared goals. With this in mind, the employee handbook should be a positive tool for encouraging growth, improving morale, and aligning employee behavior with company policies.

You may have the best leadership team in place but without an employee handbook to guide everyone along, you cannot expect harmony. Your employees and even your managers must have something to instruct and guide them so they know they are doing everything "by the book." As a boss, you cannot expect someone to follow what the "book" says if they do not have a "book" to follow. Amazingly enough, some bosses do just that: accuse an employee of failure to follow rules and procedures that are nonexistent.

The tone of the handbook should be positive throughout. The introduction can set this tone by using a friendly letter from the company president in which the general mission or long-term goals of the business are outlined. When practical, explain the reasoning behind specific policies, especially those that may be controversial.

It may surprise you to find out it really takes a short time to write a handbook after you have gathered the information. In fact, you can generally write one in less than an hour by following suggestions in this book for suitable content for your company.

As you are planning what you want to include, flip through this guide for some ideas before you read it cover to cover. Jot down some notes on things you know you need to address. What areas are giving you the greatest problems? Where are the most disturbing issues? What is proving to be a problem for you or your employees? What questions do you answer repeatedly? Afterward, you will be ready to start your manual and go through this book page by page.

To understand the various purposes of a handbook, one option is to look at those used by other companies. Ask your spouse, best friend, or another business owner for their company's handbook, remembering that rather than simply adopting what works for another operation, you will need to tailor the contents to reflect your own policies, corporate culture, procedures, and type of business. A construction company may emphasize workplace safety while a law firm may want to stress honesty and integrity, for example. If you know the reason you need a handbook, you are ready to start making notes.

Pull ideas from leaders within your company. Ask for input and then begin to plan your handbook using this guide. Have a few of your leaders in the company take a look at this book so they have a good idea of what you are trying to accomplish.

After you have the employee handbook in place, you will not only offer a better way for your leaders to manage the employees but you will also provide security to your employees and supervisors. They will feel that they are able to count on you for fair and honest dealings. If everyone feels they are treated equally, you will avoid discrimination lawsuits and many everyday problems.

Most employee-employer relationships can be discharged "at will," but some cannot be discharged "at will" because of pending lawsuits and other complications. Some employees will find a loophole to crawl through when they are discharged, and they may regain their jobs if there is no handbook in place explaining that the relationship between the employer and employee is an "at will" relationship. We will help you leave nothing to chance.

Your employee handbook should be an extension of you but not a replacement for your active voice in your company. You cannot give your managers or employees your handbook and expect them to follow it without ever wanting to hear from you directly. They want to hear they are doing a good job from time to time. If they are not doing something the way you would expect them to do it, they would like to hear it directly from you. They want to hear you tell them that policies and procedures are being followed, and they want to know of any changes straight from the boss and not just as an addendum to a handbook, although the addendum is necessary, too.

As a word of caution, remember as you are writing your handbook that policies and procedures that back up your handbook should be enforced as rules and regulations that you intend to follow. The handbook will be viewed as the communication tool for the company's policies, and you and everyone in the company will be expected to follow them. Management is expected, therefore, to commit to practice the rules you introduce.

Keep the wording easy to understand while keeping the material focused on your company goals, policies, and guidelines. Make it a positive addition to your company. Set a tone you want your employees to understand. Be upbeat and express to the workforce you are a team and you are glad each one of the employees has chosen to become a crucial part of a strong and amicable community.

WHY YOUR COMPANY NEEDS AN EMPLOYEE HANDBOOK

It is likely that your company already has many rules and regulations in effect for its employees. They may deal with whether it is acceptable to smoke in the building, where and when employees are allowed to eat lunch, or what time the employee should report to work each day.

There may be laws at the federal, state, and local level that your company is required to comply with, and perhaps you or your employees are not even aware of them. An employee handbook that is researched and properly written will help prevent legal problems that arise because someone in the company simply was not aware of a regulation that had never been communicated to them. With an employee handbook, you will have an effective means of providing that communication and protecting yourself, your company, and your employees from future problems.

Owners, managers, department heads, or human resources staff spend much of their time dealing with employee relations and relaying rules and regulations to the staff. When there are no clear, written policies on employee and company benefits, rules and regulations, the people in charge are left having to answer questions and do a learn-as-you-go type of management system. Misinformation can result in uneven and unfair application of rules and regulations throughout the organization, not to mention the amount of time and resources expended to develop rules as situations pop up. There may also be many practices your company has that employees do not know, and this means that each time an issue arises, the owner, the human resources director, or a manager has to figure out what these rules are as they go along. This practice can lead to varying rules being followed in different departments, inevitably leading to discrimination.

An employee handbook can keep you from having to reinvent the wheel every time an issue, question, or dispute arises. While it may take time to develop and implement an employee handbook, once the solid foundation is created, the handbook provides a reference for both the employer and the employee.

Documentation allows employees a "go-to" place so they can find answers when they need questions resolved in their work environment. They do not have to turn to other staff or management to answer these questions for them. The answers are already spelled out in the employee handbook so everyone can always gain quick insight to company policies when they need to know something specific.

If an employee's child becomes ill, answers to his or her questions about family medical leave are available. Perhaps an employee's spouse has to travel out of state for some reason and the employee wants to go along. He or she would need to know what the vacation policy is and whether they were eligible to take the time off to make the trip. Sometimes it can be a simple question such as, "Do employees get to take breaks during the day?" or as complex as "My supervisor said he would not promote me because I am a woman, and he wants a man in that position. Isn't that discrimination?"

When an employee asks supervisors or human resources for more information, the supervisor or HR staff can either refer the employee to the handbook or find the answer quickly in the handbook themselves. Small issues like what time the work day starts, where the break rooms are located, and what the company policy is on personal telephone calls during work hours can be addressed almost completely through an employee handbook.

Other issues, such as discrimination and legality cannot be fully addressed in an employee handbook. For those larger issues, an employee handbook can communicate the company policy on those issues and provide information on where an employee should turn for further information. You may find yourself developing policy along with a handbook.

Will everything be completely covered in the handbook? Probably not, but most items of interest should be covered. An important step to ensure that the handbook is as comprehensive as possible is to get input from everyone. So what does an employee handbook do for your company?

- Provides written documentation of the rules and regulations
- Saves time, resources, and money
- Provides communication between management and staff
- Potentially provides legal protection
- Spells out privileges and responsibilities for staff and company

As you can see, an employee handbook saves you time and provides you with peace of mind during potentially stressful times.

WHO SHOULD USE THIS GUIDE

Large or small, just starting out or continuing to grow, all businesses need clear, written documentation and communication of their vision, mission, benefits, rules, and regulations. You can follow this book without preparing ahead. Open it and you can insert your information and ideas while running with it. This book will get you started, and after you have written your own handbook, you will discover the many benefits of having one.

INFORMATION THIS GUIDE CONTAINS

We have included all the standard policies for employees and employers relating to the employee/employer relationship. You will be taken, step by step, through the process of developing employee regulations for your company as well as being provided resources for local, state, and federal employment laws.

Not all of the information provided in this guide will be necessary for every company. For example, one company may decide to have an employee smoking area, while another company may choose to ban on-site smoking. Whichever option you choose, you will be provided with sample copy and assistance in determining which policy works best for your company.

In addition, you will find information and resources to develop your company mission and vision. You will see how to relay information to employees using your company handbook. You will focus on "must haves" such as anti-discrimination regulations, cultural and company diversity policies, and American's with Disabilities Act (ADA) compliance. You will discover regulations that are required for your company and will be assisted in wording those regulations. At completion, you will have a written method of communicating with your employees—your company's own employee handbook.

THINGS YOU WILL NOT FIND IN THIS GUIDE

While this guide attempts to address all the common issues, rules, regulations, and benefits related to an employee handbook, it cannot provide information on every possible situation. No matter how well developed an employee handbook is, there will always be unexpected issues that arise. However, this guide provides a process for an employee to request information not in the handbook.

This guide is not a substitute for person-to-person communication and reinforcement of a company's rules and regulations. Communication with employees is crucial to success in business. No handbook can ever replace quality in-person communication, effective management, and staff development. An employee handbook enhances management and HR communication, but it is in no way intended to replace human interaction.

WHAT THIS GUIDE IS NOT

This book is not a substitute for legal counsel. In fact, after your handbook is complete, you are advised to take it to legal counsel for final approval before you place it in the hands of an employee. Make sure an employment attorney addresses any issues you need to include in your handbook. While this guide will provide you with resources to determine what the laws are in your area, it is important to understand that just as your employee handbook cannot address all possible employment related issues, neither can this guide provide you with all the legal information necessary for your handbook. You can retain an attorney to review your handbook for a smaller fee than you would pay fighting expensive legal battles. A small investment now can save a large payout in legal fees and problems later.

This book should not be transferred verbatim into your handbook, but it should be used to develop team communications and your own policies.

An employee handbook is not meant to take the place of a complete policies and procedures manual. It should be as general as possible about the company's benefits, culture, rules, and regulations that are true for all employees, without information on specific job functions, roles, and departmental procedures. Your company can create a complete policies and procedures manual that is specific for job functions or by department, but an employee handbook is the generic information that relates to every employee and relays employment laws and on-site rules, regulations, and procedures.

In the next section, we will get started writing your handbook. You are in for a real treat. We have prepared everything for you; all you need from this point is to supply your particular information in all the right places.

As you begin developing your handbook, you can be assured the best companies in the world have the forethought to give a handbook to their employees. Congratulations on taking this important step in the development and future of your company!

1

PREPARING TO WRITE YOUR HANDBOOK

A handbook will benefit your company only if it is tailor-made to meet the needs of your company and employees. Before you begin creating a handbook for all your employees, list the rules and guidelines you expect your employees to follow as well as any protocol you want strictly enforced.

Keep in mind as you are writing your handbook that your prospective employees are curious about the company they are going to work for: its history and its expectations, how it will handle some legal issues, its goals, and its mission statement. They want information about sick leave, PTO time, benefits, orientation periods, and training. In fact, they want to know as much as possible as quickly as possible about the company they call their employer. The handbook, after all, is to be used by the employees.

Keep your handbook simple. Before you write it, ask an attorney for suggestions for topics and language that will protect your particular enterprise legally. You do not want to throw around legal terms you know nothing about. You should not make legal statements if you have no way of knowing whether those statements apply in your area or state.

Since we want to show you how to write a handbook as simply and quickly as possible, this book includes some forms and samples you may incorporate into your handbook with slight modification.

UNDERSTANDING HOW TO USE THIS GUIDE

Go through this handbook and read all the preparatory information before proceeding with the practical details of your handbook. Make notes and lists as you go so that you will find your handbook coming together before you know it.

Just as laying a solid foundation for your business is important, so is having a solid foundation for creating your handbook. It will be the liaison between your company's management and staff, and you want it to present the best image of management as possible while providing a good company overview.

You will create your employee handbook step by step. We will begin with the "introduction" and "welcome" to new employees and provide samples and information on everything necessary all the way through discharge of employment.

You will find a checklist for determining which policies you want to include in your employee handbook, as well as sample wording of these policies and instructions for selecting which are best for your company. You will have a working employee handbook of your own designed specifically for your company.

You will learn how to distribute and implement your employee handbook. We will present record keeping issues about documenting receipt of the handbook, updating policies and regulations, and encouraging employees to use the handbook as a resource tool. You will be given a process for keeping your handbook up to date, distributing the updates, and what to do when a policy or regulation changes to ensure that your employees receive new information.

The last part of the book will help you research laws about the employer/ employee relationship. You will find in this section a directory of Web sites and government contact information for wage and labor agencies and organizations in each state.

For the most complete working employee handbook, adhere to this guide as you develop your handbook. Skipping ahead in this book or omitting a critical step can leave you with an employee handbook that is incomplete, inaccurate, or difficult for an employee to understand.

The majority of employees use an employee handbook as a resource for seeking specific information at a specific time rather than reading it cover to cover. For example, a woman who does not plan to have children for some time is not interested in how much maternity leave she has before she is hired. However, a few years down the road she may be interested in knowing about maternity leave. Where can she turn? With an employee handbook, she should be able to find the information she needs at her fingertips. She can find the forms she needs to fill out to request leave and even where to submit them. Realizing that most employees use their handbook as a reference we have written this guide by subject.

If you follow our guide from beginning to end, you will have an easy-to-use, complete resource tool that will save your business time, hassle, legal issues, and expense. Since the goal of any company is to make money to stay in business, an employee handbook is a simple, cost effective way to reduce overhead and save money.

HOW TO DETERMINE WHAT YOUR COMPANY NEEDS

The crucial part of creating an employee handbook is determining your company's specific needs. If you are the owner, ask yourself what type of environment and culture you want to foster in your business. If it is small, it could grow exponentially. Your employee handbook should be prepared to handle that growth while addressing current needs. For a larger company with an HR staff or a manager responsible for updating the handbook, its creation offers a good opportunity for senior management, HR, and key staff members to concentrate on the direction the company should take.

The handbook may be a product of upper management, parent companies, owners, and human resources staff. If so, plan to take some time to collect everyone's thoughts and share drafts.

THE CREATIVE PROCESS IN A NUTSHELL

Talk to key people, managers, and employees in your company and get their ideas about a handbook. Send out a questionnaire and ask for input. Find out areas where employees are fuzzy on company policy. Discuss what they think would be useful to see in a handbook and have someone compile all contributions.

Some companies appoint a trainer to write their handbook. If you have corporate trainers or employees in charge of orientation, involve them in the development of the handbook.

If someone else is writing the handbook, follow up on a daily basis to ensure that it has not been pushed to a back burner. In a sue-happy nation, you need to have an employee handbook in place as soon as possible. If you do not have one and have not really needed one, consider yourself lucky.

Below are suggestions to pass along to the person who is in charge of compiling information for the manual. Have them consider these points as they draft your handbook. Advise them to:

- Compile a list of questions for employees.

- Talk to every type of employee: supervisors, employees in training, and employees who have been with the company for a number of years. Find out what they need to see in the handbook and what they would like the handbook will include.

- Check old policies to select the material that should be incorporated into the new handbook.

- Talk to everyone in leadership positions and decide what points they would like to be covered.

- Talk to HR and see what issues need to be addressed to retain employees and reduce hiring and training costs.

- It is important to include brief descriptions of the company's services or its product line.

After you collect information, you will be ready to consult this tutorial and write your handbook quickly. Below are some reminders to help you keep the process simple.

- Use layman terms. Make your handbook easy to read.

- Do not elaborate on policies. Make simple statements of fact and move on.

- Be blunt. Avoid big words and elaborate explanations.

- Keep the manual simple but use terminology your workforce understands.

After the manual has been written, have key people approve it in writing before taking it to an attorney for review.

FORMAT THE HANDBOOK

With the book written, it is time to format it. The arrangement of information should make it easy to use as a reference. It is not necessary to have page numbers in your handbook if it is in a binder because you may need to add or remove a page although you may number pages in sections if you like so that updates may be done by section rather than by updating the entire booklet. If you choose to use three-ring binders, you may want to purchase those with pockets in the inside covers so you can include any additional worksheets or lists.

GETTING THE WRITTEN WORD OUT

After your attorney gives your handbook the thumbs-up, get it in front of your employees as soon as possible. Hold a leadership meeting with your management team who contributed to the handbook and ask them to review it so that they have a general understanding of it.

A few days after you have given your management time to review the manual, call a meeting with the rest of the employees and get the word out. Ask each employee to review it and raise questions about any policy or procedure. Ask all employees to sign a form (see example) acknowledging that they have read and understand the company policies and procedures or that they will do so.

HANDBOOK ACKNOWLEDGEMENT FORM

I have received a copy of [insert company name] employee handbook. I have read and understand the policies and procedures detailed in the handbook. I will read over the handbook any time I have questions about my employment and agree to uphold the guidelines for employment to the best of my ability.

I understand that anything written in the handbook has been approved by legal counsel of the company and nothing is simply implied in the handbook.

By signing below, I am stating that I agree with the company's policies and procedures and agree to follow the guidelines in the handbook provided. I understand that my employment with the company above is only "at will" and the company makes no guarantee of employment. I understand that the company can terminate my employment at any time and that I can terminate my employment at any time. Neither party will be required to give a reason or cause for the discharge. By signing below I acknowledge receipt of the company handbook and acknowledge my employment with the company is not for any set period of time.

[Employee]   Date _____

Employee Signature _____

Employee's Name Printed_____

Witness Signature_____

FORMATTING

The first impression a person forms about a company begins during orientation, and the best way to put forth a positive feeling about your company is through an employee handbook. Plus you are assured that new employees have the company's rules and policies at hand.

In most employee handbooks, the company guidelines and policies are formatted by sections and chapter notations. For example, in the first chapter, the first section would be indicated by 1:1 and the second section of the first chapter would be 1:2 for easy reference. Initially, we are not going to format the guidelines as we walk you through how to write your handbook. However, at the end of this handbook, you will be given a properly formatted sample.

THE STEPS
Step One – Assign

Determine who is going to decide what will be included in an employee handbook for your company. Ideally, you will have the cooperation of a team that implements and enforces the benefits and regulations of the handbook such as human resources director, other HR staff, executive managers, owners, CEOs, and sometimes even department managers.

At least one person should be assigned to create the handbook, and upper management or the owner should approve the proposed content to ensure that all necessary subjects are included. This is an ideal time to map the future goals, culture, and environment of the company. Assign handbook duties according to the strengths and knowledge of contributors.

Step Two – Research and Investigation

After you have selected your team and determined who is responsible for which processes, do a bit of detective work. Talk to managers and department heads about how they currently manage their departments. Doing this can be time-consuming if you have a large company, but the important part is to discover what is already working well and incorporate that into the handbook. You may find yourself changing the unwritten policy by adding a new written policy to the handbook and perhaps to a policy manual.

For example, one department manager may have no problem with employees' working half-hour lunches during the week and leaving early on Friday. Another department manager may refuse his staff this perk because of Friday deadlines. This is a clear case of inconsistent rules and regulations between departments. Another example is flex time that may be allowed in one department but not another, causing morale problems or even a legal problem: discrimination or preferential treatment. The process of creating an employee handbook can resolve issues like these.

It will be up to you to discover current practices in your company. Look for postings on company bulletin boards in employee common areas. Do they have all the legal postings required by law for a company, such as minimum wage postings, equal employment, and anti-discrimination notices?

Review company memos and newsletters to find the policies, rules, and regulations that have been issued in written form, although not in an employee handbook. Review past employee complaints and how they were resolved to get a good idea of what the company decided was the best course of action so that you can put forth regulations consistent with the company's past decisions.

Another good resource is to interview or survey managers about how they already handle certain situations. A survey will help you discover if there are policies and regulations in force that are consistent (or inconsistent). You can construct the interviews and questionnaires or surveys so they fall in line with your company's vision or mission for consistency of purpose.

Your survey or questions might include the following:

- What are the procedures for time keeping and time sheets for payroll?

- What are the pay periods and pay dates?

- How much and when are vacation and sick leave accrued and available to be taken?

- What are the eligibility requirements for health insurance (if provided) and how does an employee apply for this benefit?

- Is the company required to offer FMLA leave?

- What is the policy on maternity leave and paternity leave?

- What are the benefits that the company offers to employees? What are the eligibility requirements for these benefits?

- What are any other policies or HR/payroll regulations required by law or offered to all employees by the company that should be included?

Surveys work well with staff also but use paper for anonymity. Some employees may fear a reprisal for honestly telling you their thoughts about a policy. An anonymous paper survey would allow for openness.

Your company's current personnel manual or policy and procedures manuals are a good place to look for current company information. Ask department heads, supervisors, and HR department heads to divulge the reasons people have recently been discharged. Is it something the company could have prevented?

When you have compiled current practices, allow your sources to review your draft to clarify any ambiguities.

Step Three – Putting It All Together

Now that you have the information, decide which policies will be included in your employee handbook.

Begin with the first policy in this guide, match that up to the information you have compiled, and using the checklist included in a later chapter of this guide, check off the policies you want to include in your book and how you want those policies carried out. The checklist is critical for you as it will be your guide through Section Two of your handbook, helping you determine which policies to review more in depth and which to discard.

For example, you may decide to include "Smoking Policy" on your list. This guide includes possible terminology: "Smoking is Allowed," "Smoking is Not Allowed," or "Smoking is allowed only in designated areas." An excerpt from the worksheet would look something like this:

_____13.4   Smoking Policy (Select the policy to include)

_____Smoking is allowed

_____Smoking is not allowed

_____Smoking is allowed in designated areas

Comments:

_____

_____

If you want to include a smoking policy, check the "Smoking Policy," and then select the type of smoking policy you need. In the comments, you can write any notes for yourself about what you want to say about the smoking policy you have selected.

For example, if you selected "Smoking allowed only in designated areas," your comment would be something like this: during breaks only (see break policy) and only in the employee break room on the south side of the building.

Comments are a note for yourself, so that you have everything together that you need by using this guide and the checklist, avoiding having to go back and forth through the notes you have compiled.

This checklist will be used in the next step when you begin to write your company's employee handbook. If you selected "Smoking is allowed only in designated areas," you would turn to that policy in this book for sample wording and write your policy.

Step Four – Write the Handbook

After you have compiled all the information and completed your checklist, you will be ready to write the policies you have selected.

Step Five – Reviewing and Approval

At this step, you should have a completed employee handbook with all the policies written and all the blank forms attached ready for review. Do a thorough edit and a final check of all the content to ensure that you have included everything necessary for your employees.

Run your edited copy past the HR department and the payroll department for review of any of their policies in the employee handbook. Then your supervisor, the owner, the CEO, or the manager who is in charge of the company should review the entire handbook and approve the policies. The final stop is the employment attorney.

Step Six – Final Proof and Distribute

After the attorney or legal advisor has reviewed the handbook, make those changes, perform a final edit, proofread the document, and distribute it to your employees. We will discuss distributing your handbook later in this guide.

So there you have it, all the steps necessary to write your employee handbook. It is an easy process to follow and if you are dedicated to providing your employees with a "go-to" place to get their questions answered, you should be glad to get this project completed in record time!

We will review in more depth all the information you need to compile before sitting down to write your employee handbook. So now that you have your surveys, questionnaires, and interviews in front of you, you are ready to write your handbook.

2

WRITE YOUR EMPLOYEE HANDBOOK

Finally, you are at the point of creation! You will be excited to know the employee handbook you create will include time-saving information for your employees, enabling your key people to be more productive. Everything you include in your handbook will allow your employees to find the information they need when they need it.

PREPARING TO CREATE

It is time to focus on the handbook's introduction. You are introducing a new employee to the company. You are introducing existing employees to the goals, culture, vision, and mission of the company. This is your chance to present the company in the best possible light. Describe the company environment and let the employee know about the dress code and character of the company. For example, your handbook might state something like "At Comic Books, Ltd., we strive to provide a relaxed atmosphere. Dress is always casual."

You need to have the following information available to you.

- Company Information
- Background and History

- Mission Statement or Company Motto
- Company Directory or HR Contact Information
- Copies of Existing Policies and Procedures
- Copies of Existing Company Standard Forms

Having these documents handy, along with the questionnaires, surveys, and any other research information you obtained by following the previous steps in this guide, you should be ready to start your list of handbook contents.

In this chapter you will find a policy checklist for your use. It will help you organize all the information you now have and turn it into a cohesive and functional employee handbook. Feel free to make copies of this checklist for your convenience in selecting the policies and sections to put in your handbook.

Take time to compile as much company history and background as possible and then summarize it using the key points. A company mission statement is a succinct way to give employees an understanding of the purpose of your company. If your company does not have one, speak to the person in charge, presenting possible wording for review.

Mission statements are usually short and direct, aiming for the most superlative possible goals. For example, "XYZ, Inc., is dedicated to producing the best (name of product), using the finest resources, the most energy efficient, environmentally friendly, up-to-date technology in the field for our customers' highest satisfaction." Sometimes the wording is the product of the board of directors, the owner, or even stockholders. Make sure that no one who might wish to contribute is left out of the creative process, as it may turn out to be a historic document.

I once sat through a four-hour board meeting session on this one item on the agenda—wording a state agency's mission statement. It was quite a serious process. Thirteen directors spent one hour on the spelling of "ensure," whether it was "ensure" or "insure." When the

> 22 words were finally approved (with "ensure"), copies were made on imitation onionskin paper that looked like the yellowed U.S. Declaration of Independence, then framed, and hung up in every department and reprinted in every agency publication.
>
> —Former Commonwealth of Pennsylvania Information Specialist

If your company is in the throes of developing a mission statement or a concisely stated vision that would be included in your handbook, consider the following phrases meant to inspire employees with somewhat uplifting language and a common goal.

- A positive attitude and image
- Skilled, knowledgeable, and dedicated employees
- Ease of obtaining service
- Flexibility of service
- Easy communication
- Responsiveness to customer requests
- Keeping the customer informed
- Completing quality projects on time

Even if you have a current policies and procedures manual in place, you may want to use it only as a guide rather than summarizing it. Refer to it but do not simply re-write it.

Remember, ideally, you will give the handbook to all employees. Sure, your current employees already know much of the information you will include in the handbook, but it should reflect the company's general policies, rules, and regulations while providing company history and mission statement.

- Introduction
- This section contains:
- Welcome to the Company – Samples
- Introduction to the Company and Company History

- Where did the company come from?
- Discipline
- How to Use Your Employee Manual
- Disclaimer
- Organizational Chart
- General purpose and legal protection
- Location of Employment Related Postings

It is crucial that the introduction set a warm, inviting conversational tone. How an employer presents the opening of the handbook will determine how well the employee receives—or whether they take the time to read—the handbook. As the handbook progresses, it will deal with unpleasant issues such as violence in the workplace, filing complaints, and discrimination statutes. These harsher policies in the handbook will be received much better if the tone is initially friendly.

Use simple terms without being too informal. Consider the introduction to the employee handbook as a pleasant welcome and guide the employee by providing the information needed to be successful in the company. You want your employees to view the handbook as an orientation to the company, and later, as a reference for answers to common questions or issues that may arise.

Keeping this in mind, you are ready to create the first section of the employee handbook—the introduction.

At this point provide a short summary of the company to serve as a highlight of sections to come: the company history and the vision and mission statements. When you add your own specific information in this section, be sure to keep it brief, no more than one page, since its purpose is to welcome the employee and give a glimpse into what to expect from the rest of the employee handbook.

When a new employee starts with your company, the one section he or she is most likely to read all the way through will be the welcomes that provides some background information on the company in an interesting and informative manner.

WELCOME TO THE COMPANY—SAMPLES

Your introduction may be a friendly welcome statement. Take a look at these samples:

Welcome to [Insert Name of Company]

We are glad you have chosen to join us. We are a company striving to deliver great customer service while maintaining outstanding employer-employee relations. We know the key to our success is our employees. Therefore, we make every effort to make you feel at home here from the beginning.

This handbook covers our company history, mission, and overall goals. Please use it as a resource for benefits we provide our employees as well as our policies and procedures.

Again, Welcome to [Insert name of company]

[Insert signature of president or owner]

Include information about the environment the employee should expect by working with the company. Consider this, for example:

Welcome Aboard!

We are glad you have chosen to affiliate with [insert name of company]. We strive to deliver great customer service while maintaining friendly employer-employee relations. We know the key to our success is in our employees. Therefore, we make every effort to make you feel at home here from the beginning.

[Insert name of company] was conceived for building homes from the ground up using quality materials. Since 1979, we have been using the best lumber and other materials to ensure our homes are top of the line. We have built our business on honest communications with our customers and our employees.

Our employees know we are here for them. We have an open-door policy. Let us know whenever you have questions or concerns.

In this handbook you will find our company history, our mission, and our goals. Please refer to the handbook for the benefits we provide our employees as well as our policies and procedures.

Again, Welcome to [insert name of company]

[Insert signature of president or owner]

Welcome to [Insert Name of Company]!

We are pleased to welcome you and hope your will find your position and duties here pleasant, challenging, and rewarding. Our staff are some of the most talented and creative individuals in the industry, and we are proud to welcome you to our team.

Please take the time to review this section of your employee handbook where we will provide you with some company background information, history, our vision and mission, and introduce you to our culture and environment so you can feel more comfortable and better understand the nature of your new workplace.

We are excited to have you aboard and look forward to a successful and productive working relationship. Congratulations on your new career with [insert name of company].

INTRODUCTION TO THE COMPANY AND COMPANY HISTORY

Corporate "culture" is the buzzword meaning a company's internal working environment that contributes to its competitive edge in attracting talented employees. Your company needs to promote its vision, mission, goals, culture, and rich history to applicants and current employees, so they feel honored to be a part of the company.

A company's mission is key to setting the path that employees will follow. In this second section of the new employee's introduction to the company, insert the company's vision and mission statement clearly putting forth the company's beliefs, values, and goals as more than theory. They should be presented as a solid reality and a foundation upon which the company is based and which each employee strives to advance in day-to-day duties. Everything an employee does should carry forth the company mission, striving to improve, expedite, and streamline every task.

The next part of this section is your opportunity to inform your new employees of the history of your company. Using a conversational, upbeat, positive tone, explain how your company was founded, its roots, the past and potential growth of the company, any major changes that have occurred, and anything to help the employee understand where the company wants to go.

Include dates, names, anecdotes, and company lore. List milestones in growth, changes and adaptations to the market, innovations, laws that affected production, people who personally made a difference, employees who moved from the bottom to the top of the company, voluntary contributions to the community, environmental commitments, record production years, launches of successful products, increased efficiency achieved by individual employees who were rewarded, annual awards banquets with the categories of awards, photos of memorable occasions or previous (smaller) buildings that the company occupied, or ribbon cutting and ground-breaking events. If nothing is already written, most companies have a long-time, self-appointed historian who can help you construct a short history that can also be used in annual reports, newsletters, and publicity. You will find that a brief timeline of the company's history will be a good addition to your other publications as well, such as newsletters and annual reports.

Karen White started this home care company with one goal in mind: to provide excellent service to people who were used to receiving less than adequate customer relations. With a commitment to provide great service, she knew her customer base would grow from day one, and it has grown to a force of more than 100 employees in less than three years.

At Karen White, Ltd., we believe we have a service that people need, and we give our customers excellent service while keeping a reasonable price the average person can afford. We want our customers to have a smile when we leave them, and we give many less fortunate people reason to smile.

Caring for elderly people is not always easy, but we have proven it can be affordable. We believe great customer care is the reason we are successful, and we make sure our clients and their families are well satisfied with their in-home care.

Karen White employees dress for success, but they dress comfortably. They are well groomed and relaxed so that most of our clients feel at home with us from the moment we meet. We like the feeling we get when we meet our clients, and we continue to grow because we like our jobs. We are individuals committed to providing employees a good job with flexibility.

We are here for the working parent and ready to make schedule changes so you can keep your children the focus of your world, but when you are on a job, we want your client to be your focus.

If you are the boss, you get to set the tone for your handbook. From the introduction to the policies themselves, you have control of the nature of your message and the information you wish to convey. The way to make the development of the manual easier is to keep sight of the things you want to pass along to your employee. Imagine you are on a podium talking to all the employees. You only have one chance to say what you want to say and then you can never discuss it again. What would you say? What do you want people to know about your company? Think about it and then say everything you need to say.

Other Ideas to Consider for Your Introduction

- What do you think is most important for the employee to know about your company?

- What do you think all of your employees want to know about the company's goals or history?

- Why do you have your particular mission statement?

- What kind of atmosphere will the employee find at the company?

- What service does the company provide?

- Does the company provide a product? If so, why is it better than competing products?

WHERE DID THE COMPANY COME FROM?—SAMPLES

After you have briefly described the company, it is time to move onto the history of the company.

Roots are important. Everyone wants to know their own personal history as well as the history of the companies where they work. They like to speak about their jobs intelligently when asked. They want to take an active interest in their place of employment and this is your chance to provide background information about the company and instill pride in its employees.

When providing the company's history, give facts in the form of a story. Personalize the history so employees will feel more connected to the company. Provide insight and use a friendly tone.

Carl sold his first car on October 3, 1976. Of course, he didn't really have a business yet, but his first sale was a Ford Mustang that had belonged to his father. Carl used the money from the sale to open his doors with only three used cars on the lot. He used to say, "We all have to start somewhere and I just decided I would start small."

At Carl Motors, we know our humble beginnings, and we appreciate every customer we have the opportunity to serve. We cherish our customer base and know it takes more than a good car and great sales pitch to keep us in business. It takes ongoing service so that customers come back. We are dedicated to quality cars and great service. When someone comes in to our dealership with a small down payment, we find a way to put them in the car they want. After all, "We all have to start somewhere." At Carl Motors, we will always be sure our customers are happy they came to us.

Of course, your employee handbook should be specific to your company, so do add your own flair. Take the time to think about what the company really needs to relay to the employee.

When writing the company history, include the past values your company has demonstrated while stating the goals for the future.

HOW TO USE YOUR EMPLOYEE MANUAL

As the title of this section suggests, this is where you will tell your employee two important things: the purpose of their employee handbook and how to use it effectively.

Indicate here that there is an expectation for them to read the handbook. We recommend adding a form to this section (see Appendix for a sample form) that the employee is required to sign that will be kept in their employee file that states they received, read, and understand all the information contained in their employee handbook. No one will have an excuse for not following the handbook's guidelines. It provides a fallback defense whenever an employee requires discipline. When letting an employee go, non-adherence to a policy in the handbook is grounds for dismissal. Should the company be sued by a former or current employee, the handbook and the employee's signed statement affirming that they received and read the handbook provide stronger legal protection than someone's word alone.

Please refer to the Sample Employee Handbook in the back of this book for suggested language for this section of your handbook.

Human resources may be the "go to" place in your company (a good idea to avoid having supervisors sidetracked by repetitive employment-related inquiries). If so, the handbook is the place to make clear that employees who do not find answers in the handbook should speak to someone in HR.

Here is an example of such a statement.

> If you have any questions regarding policy, employment, regulations, or benefits, please check this handbook for answers. If you need specific information not covered in the handbook, please see (insert name of person) in the Human Resources Department.

If your human resources department's duties are limited to completing paperwork rather than dealing directly with employees, supervisors must be ready to provide employment answers, a situation that makes a handbook a must for consistency and nondiscrimination in the workplace. Should a circumstance arise where supervisors are misinforming employees, this is the opportune occasion to settle on one policy and either create a handbook or amend the one in place.

DISCLAIMER

This section should include a disclaimer. This is suggested wording.

> The information in this employee handbook and its properly filed and distributed updates supersede all verbal information relayed to the employee. If the employee has been given verbal instructions that conflict with this employee handbook, the employee handbook is the final authority on the company policy, and the employee should adhere to all policies in the employee handbook at all times.
>
> Your attorney may wish to amend or apply stronger language to such a statement.

While you are selecting the information for your handbook, remember to include a disclaimer that the handbook does not constitute a contract for employment. Employee handbooks, if not properly worded and developed, can indeed be interpreted as legal and binding in a court of law. It is important that the policies be accurate and based on applicable laws for your area. The disclaimer should further deal with areas not covered by the handbook, such as, "This list (of reasons for discipline, for example, or 'This handbook') is intended as an example only and is not intended to indicate all acts by an employee that could lead to employee discipline." With this statement, you can avoid having an employee contest discharge because the handbook did not specifically list "stealing" as a reason for dismissal. If you create a list of activities that will result in discharge, be sure to let your employees know that this is not an exclusive list and that you always reserve the right to decide to terminate a worker's employment.

With this statement and other information that supports it, you will make it clear to the employee that the handbook cannot possibly cover all eventualities during their employment with the company, but that the company has a system in place for those issues not specifically covered in the handbook. This system could be as simple as giving the new employee the name of the human resources director or contact personnel, or by having the employee follow a chain of command beginning with their immediate supervisor and then moving upward from there until the issue is resolved.

Another warning when writing a handbook is not to use restrictive language. Words such as "will," "must," or "in all cases" may bind employers to actions they did not want to take in a given case. Collective bargaining jargon like "terms and conditions of employment" or "seniority" also could be interpreted as creating an employment contract.

With the introductory section of the handbook it is important not to step outside the lines of an employee/employer relationship and include something that might limit your ability to maintain an employee "at will" status. More information will be provided on employment "at will" status in the next section of the handbook.

ORGANIZATION CHART

This is an optional section of your handbook. An organizational chart is a good idea for any company to have on hand along with a procedure for updates, because it shows the employee the chain of command and the flow of information and approvals. A new employee cannot immediately know everyone else in the company so an organizational chart helps to place unfamiliar people in the appropriate job functions.

An "org chart" tells a new employee where to go for a customer service related inquiry, or who is responsible for shipping and receiving, or even who their immediate supervisor is and how the chain of command flows from that level. This is not a bad idea for existing employees as well, since staff may not know who performs what function in other departments.

The telephone call list is especially helpful for larger companies with many employees. It is hard to keep track of all the changes, additions, and deletions as employees come, go, get transferred, resign, or achieve promotion. For a new employee, having a telephone call list for employees and being able to match that to the organizational chart is a valuable tool to aid them until they become familiar with the other staff in the company. Because it changes often in a large company, you may want these pages to be provided separately for posting or to use a binder for the entire handbook.

GENERAL PURPOSE AND LEGAL PROTECTION

The purpose of your handbook needs to be stated in the introduction. You should make sure you mention the full purpose of the handbook while stating there is no guarantee of employment outside the employee's current shift. Take a look at the example below.

The purpose of this handbook is to explain our company. We want to explain where we have been and where we plan to go in the future. We want our employees to understand our history as well as our future plans.

We expect all of our employees to read this handbook and to follow our rules and regulations as a guideline that we have put into effect. If you ever need further guidance or if you have questions you feel are left unanswered, please talk to your manager or see someone in Human Resources for more information.

The handbook can change at any time. If there are policy changes, a memo is given to the supervisors to pass the information to all employees.

If a policy change is implemented at any time and you have questions, please do not hesitate to ask. It is important that you understand all our policies and procedures.

One of the purposes of a handbook is to protect the company from a legal standpoint. Therefore, you will need to keep your handbook up to date as a way of leading by example.

In the introduction, you want to be sure you encourage your employees to direct their complaints and their questions to the appropriate person. Let employees know what procedures they should follow to make and resolve complaints. Designate several people in the company to receive employee complaints and state that there will be no retaliation against any employee for filing a complaint. Having—and enforcing—a written complaint procedure can help shield your business from liability if an employee later sues for illegal harassment or discrimination.

We strongly urge you to include the Handbook Acknowledgement Form that will cover you and your company should there ever be an issue of employee compliance. Employees, in many cases, must sign the form before they can clock in for their first shift.

LOCATION OF EMPLOYMENT RELATED POSTINGS

Employees will become accustomed to checking bulletin boards for special company announcements, helpful information, overtime shifts, company parties, legal notices, policy changes, and company meetings.

You should address how employees may use company bulletin boards. Following is a sample to use in addressing the issue of bulletin boards.

Our company relays information through the use of company bulletin boards located near all time clocks. Please get into the habit of checking these bulletin boards for important information when you clock in. These boards are crucial for communication throughout the plant. Postings are to be done by supervisors only.

Remove the last sentence above and adapt the following to allow employees to post information on bulletin boards.

> If you have information you would like to communicate to all employees, please present it to (name of person) in the (name of department) for approval and posting for a limited period.

Be sure to notify anyone mentioned in the handbook, such as the person named above, that they are expected to fulfill certain duties.

Most states require certain employment related notices to be posted visibly in the workplace where the employees regularly congregate. Notices may include federal minimum wage laws, equal opportunity/nondiscrimination laws, workplace safety precautions, payroll and pay period information, and other legal or regulatory information. Review the Appendix for information about laws regarding posting information in your location.

Some companies also like to add fun things to their bulletin board or employee update location such as birthday announcements, employee achievements and awards, department achievements, meeting dates and times, and training opportunities.

If your company does not have a bulletin board, it may still be required to meet mandatory federal posting requirements, so your policy should, at a minimum, state where these mandatory postings can be found.

3

EMPLOYMENT IS "AT WILL"

The issue you need to cover at this point is called the "at will" policy which means, through common law, that employers have the right to terminate employees, without cause, and for any reason or no reason at all, provided it is not in violation of any protected or anti-discriminatory laws, and the employer is not required to give notice or provide any additional compensation to the employee should they exercise this right. At the same time, the employee is also free to terminate employment without repercussions or notice, at any time. It is a policy that enables an employee to resign for any reason, at any time, without any warning. It also allows the employer to let the employee go at any time, for any reason, and without any warning or notice. Companies that adopt this policy have documentation of their policy affording them protection from lawsuits.

Normally, the courts side with employers based on the assumption of "at-will" employment. If an employee is hired under a contract, it is legal and binding and the "at will" clause is no longer in effect.

The reason you want to address the "at-will" clause in your handbook is because of implied consent. For instance, if you have an employee who loses his job and is angry about it, he may claim someone in management promised him a job for a set length of time. Unless the handbook includes "at will," the employer would have no legal recourse.

THE "AT-WILL" POLICY

Unless your company specifically offers hiring contracts to its employees or your company is unionized, there are several good reasons for adding the "Employment At Will" policy to your handbook. Unless your company specifically offers hiring contracts to its employees or your company is unionized, you may want to consider adding the "Employment At Will" policy to your handbook. Hiring contracts will spell out the specifics of the employee-employer relationship and should include discharge and separation from employment. If your employees are unionized, you really do not need an employee handbook at all. The union will provide all the information related to the employee-employer relationship, and the company will need to focus more on policy and procedures guidelines instead.

Otherwise, this policy warrants its own section in your employee handbook. It is important because while you want your employees to feel they are a valued part of your team, you do not want them to feel as if they cannot be discharged at any time. They need to know they have no guarantee of an ongoing job with your company.

Many states currently have laws concerning "at-will" employment. It is an important protection for any company to have. Without "at-will" employment in effect, an employer must show "good cause," meaning that the employer has to prove the employee has violated some company policy to justify discharge, and that the policy used to terminate the employee was clearly indicated to the employee prior to their discharge. Without proof, the company may find itself on the losing end of a wrongful discharge lawsuit.

That is not to say that you cannot be sued you if you have used your "at will" status to terminate the employee, but it does mean that you are less likely to lose the court battle if you have promulgated your employment "at will" status. To do so you should avoid any type of language, either written or verbal, that might be construed to be a contract or promise of continued employment. Employers certainly want long-term relationships with employees because they reduce training costs, lower turnover, improve morale, and provide valuable experience. However, there are always unforeseen circumstances prompting an employer or an employee to terminate the relationship. When this happens it is important to understand that if your company has chosen not to offer hiring contracts or extending a contract or a promise of employment to the employee, the employee is considered "employed at will."

The employee handbook can spell out requirements for the employee to qualify for certain benefits upon leaving the company What this means is that perhaps the company pays all sick leave days accrued to the employee upon discharge of employment without cause. The company does have the right to state that for the employee to be eligible for this benefit, the employee must give two weeks written notice upon leaving the company. While the employee is free to leave at any time for any reason without repercussions, the employee must follow protocol and adhere to company policies to receive the benefits offered in a voluntary discharge.

"At will" protection clearly seems to favor the employer, but there are certain requirements that do have to be met before the employer can use "at will" protection in letting an employee go. For example, the employer should be certain that there is no violation of an anti-discrimination law when terminating an employee. Anti-discrimination laws can include but are not limited to:

- Age
- Race
- Religion
- Gender
- Creed
- National origin
- Sometimes sexual orientation

- The Whistleblower Act
- Active military status or past military/veterans status
- Refusal to violate company policies or wage and labor laws

NOTE: Sexual orientation is not a federally protected status; however, some states do have legislation to protect employment discrimination on this basis, and some employers choose to add this clause to their own anti-discrimination policies.

The first few points will be covered later in this handbook. The Whistleblower Act is a federal law that protects employees from being wrongfully discharged or otherwise discriminated against for reporting their employer for wrongdoing.

You can head off adverse publicity and possible lawsuits by assuring would-be whistleblowers that their complaints will be dealt with effectively in-house, if indeed, that is the case. Employers get in trouble when they discipline whistleblowers or workers who complain of harassment, discrimination, or unsafe working conditions. Your company should take action to deal with the problem itself, not with the employee who brought the problem to your attention.

There are also laws to protect employees from being pressured into performing work for less than premium pay, from having to work overtime without overtime pay, or from discrimination against the employee for military involvement, past or present. You should research state laws and city ordinances as well as your company policies before you compose this section of your handbook.

The main goal of your "at will" policy is to ensure you are able to fire employees when you want to fire them without any risk of being sued. If you provide your employee with a handbook clearly stating an "at-will" policy, the employee cannot argue that an implied contract is in place, a common practice.

Even if yours is a company with a reputation for keeping long-term employees, an "at-will" policy is protection for you and your company should the need ever arise for you to fire an employee you do not want associated with your company. Some employers hesitate to incorporate an "at-will" policy especially if they are just writing their handbook. However, the "at-will" policy can be presented to long-standing employees as a way to protect their interests as well. Here is a sample:

Employment with the Cracker Shack is "at-will." We are glad you have chosen to work for our company. We think you are a great match for Cracker Shack and hope you will enjoy working for us. However, if you choose to discontinue your working relationship with us at any time, we want you to know you are free to do so without any notice. You can leave our employ whenever you like without giving any reason. You can provide notice or you do not have to provide one if you do not feel you can. However, an "at-will" policy allows The Cracker Shack to act accordingly. If we feel we need to terminate our working relationship at any time, we can without any notice or given cause.

Furthermore, no employee or manager of the Cracker Shack has permission to change this policy. In the event of a change in the "at will" policy, the employee and owners will decide on a better contract for employment and will sign a contract to be notarized.

Nothing in this manual is a commitment to an ongoing working relationship between the employee and the Cracker Shack.

WHY THE "AT-WILL" POLICY IS CRUCIAL

Everyone needs to implement the "at-will" policy because it protects the employer. Even if some employees are able to secure contracts for ongoing employment, the "at-will" policy is generally a good practice because the employee-employer relationship is under absolutely no obligation to continue.

If rumors circulate in regard to "at-will" employment, inform your employees that they are working "at-will." Perhaps it is not clearly stated in a policies and procedures manual or an existing employee handbook; nonetheless, they are working "at-will." In the case of your policy, you are simply stating it rather than implying it by providing the employee with the necessary information regarding their employment.

CHANGES AND EXCEPTIONS

If you have someone who administers the "at will" policy, you need to provide the person's name to employees. It is usually an HR employee or the CEO, or in small companies, the owner.

MORE INFORMATION TO PROTECT THE COMPANY

Handbook Acknowledgement Form

This form is to be signed by all new employees of the Cracker Shack. As an employee of the Cracker Shack, you are stating you have read and received a copy of the Cracker Shack Employee Handbook. You are further stating you understand all the written statements in the handbook about your employment.

You understand your employment is "at-will" which means either party, you or the Cracker Shack, can dissolve the working relationship without any notice or cause. You understand the Cracker Shack makes no guarantee of employment and by signing below, you agree and accept the terms of your employment as "at-will" employment.

_____   _____
Employee Signature   Date

_____
Employee Printed Name

_____
Supervisor Signature

_____
Supervisor Printed Name

_____
Witness Signature

_____
Witness Printed Name

There are many reasons it is wise to obtain the employee's signature to indicate that no information for the employee was merely implied so that you have legal protection from suits brought by a disgruntled ex-employee. If the employee signs off on the "at-will" clause to employment within your company, he or she is admitting he knows he is working for the company "at-will." On the previous page is another sample acknowledgement form for your convenience.

It is a good idea to have a place for a supervisor to sign as well while another supervisor witnesses the signing of the "at-will" form. Remember, everyone is sue-happy; do not give your ex-employees any reason to sue you. Make sure you have an "at-will" policy that is enforceable.

Keep in mind the time it takes to read the manual. Generally, a large corporation will have the handbook covered in the first few days of orientation or training as we recommend. Be sure to ask for signatures to acknowledge the employee read or will read the handbook which covers the "at-will" policy. Forms and acknowledgements should be signed and turned in before the employee's first shift.

DO YOU NEED THIS POLICY?

If you work with contractors only or if your employees are unionized, this policy and handbook are not required, since there is no employee-employer relationship. Your company may decide to hire based on a contract, with hiring and discharge clauses written into the contract.

If yours is a small business with few employees, there is a chance you do not want to have an "at will" clause. Perhaps your employees are more like family to you, and you do not see a potential for future staff growth to necessitate an at will" policy. That is okay, but consider that without an "at will" policy, you will be required to show cause for terminating an employee, or else you could suffer legal repercussions. "Cause" or "good cause" is legal jargon that means you must have a reason for discharge that does not violate laws against discrimination. Typically, you will have to produce documentation of progressive discipline and show that the employee somehow violated a company policy—usually the ones spelled out in this employee handbook you are creating.

If you think you may not need this policy, you probably do not understand its value. The "at-will" policy is your way out if you have an employee whom you want off the premises at once. If you are sure someone has stolen merchandise from you, but you cannot prove it, you want them gone immediately. You need this policy to ensure you are protected when you no longer want to be affiliated with a certain employee.

We will examine some sample text for your "at-will" policy, and then we will discuss this policy a bit more in depth, because it really is that important to understand. See the following sample.

Employment is "At Will"

We are pleased to welcome you to our company and hope that your employment here will be a rewarding and positive experience.

[Insert company name] is committed to your success in our workplace and we want to help you continue to grow and be satisfied with your working environment; however, we cannot make any promises or guarantees for continued employment with out company.

[Insert company name] is an "at will" employer and, therefore, your employment here is "at will" meaning that you are able to resign from your position at any time, and for any reason or no reason at all, without any further requirements or recrimination, just as the company is also free to terminate employment at any time and for any reason or no reason, without any notices—with or without cause.

No part of this employee handbook constitutes, in any way, a contract or promise or guarantee of continued employment.

Now, if your company does hire someone on contract, such as senior-level management, those employees would be exempt from the employment "at will" clause in your policies.

It is also important to spell out exactly what and who can change the status of the employment "at will" relationship with an employee. See the following sample.

It is not possible for any employee to authorize a change in the employment "at will" status or to contract with any employee for terms of employment in violation of this "at will" policy without specific written consent and approval of the hiring contract by (insert highest level of management who can negotiate a contract with an employee—might also insert HR director's name as a second authorized signature).

[Insert name of company] does offer hiring packages and hiring contracts to certain senior level executive exempt management positions. For those hiring contracts, the terms and conditions of employment are defined in your contract. In the absence of this hiring contract, employment is considered "at will," and the terms of this handbook and this policy apply.

Terms such as, "We wish to have a long and fruitful employment relationship with you" or "Welcome to our family. We hope you will be with us for years to come" should be strictly avoided. It is understood that these phrases are welcoming, warm, and inviting; however, they may put the company in a legal position of having made a promise of continued employment to the employee. This is another reason to have an attorney or legal advisor review your handbook before distributing it to your employees.

4

EMPLOYEE INFORMATION

Employees should be expected to have questions. Though your employee handbook should cover most of the items a new employee needs to know, it will not take the place of training from an individual who knows the company.

The handbook should address company policies and issues and should provide a general understanding of the company and what the company needs its employees to know. It should offer the new employee a solid introduction to the company while serving as a reference tool to the current employees.

ORIENT THE EMPLOYEE

An orientation or a good training period is worth its weight in gold. From small mom-and-pop type businesses to major corporations, the orientation period is a time for you to set the tone for employees, and it helps your new employees become familiar with company procedures and meet key members of your team.

In the orientation, employees will be interested in knowing more about the payroll department, scheduling, PTO, and other benefits. An orientation period is ideal for the new employee to take the opportunity to meet other people they will be working with at the company as well as having the opportunity to ask questions. Orientation is the perfect time to go over the handbook and have new employees sign an acknowledgement of receipt of the handbook and that they understand their employment is an "at-will."

Conversely, you need to cover the orientation process in your handbook. Take a look at the sample wording used below.

> New employee orientation is critical to your success here at the Cracker Shack. You will have an orientation meeting during the first week of your employment. You will gather information by attending this meeting and discover more about the policies and procedures of the Cracker Shack. At the meeting, you will complete all forms and other paperwork needed for your employee file. We will ask you to review your benefits package as well as supply emergency contact numbers.
>
> The meeting is for our employees to ask questions and get answers. If you find you have questions as we are going through the training period or the orientation meeting, please do not hesitate to ask anything you need to know.

In this section of the handbook, you should list the company trainer's name or the person in HR who handles the orientation meeting so that the employees have a point of contact should they have questions before or after the orientation meeting.

ORIENTATION PHASE

Considered a probationary period of sorts, the orientation enables employees to see whether they like working for the company, and it allows supervisors to test whether the employee is a good match as well. The orientation period is the opportunity for an employee to begin consistent and long-term employment. Remember to adhere to the wording "orientation" or introductory period" rather than "probation" as it implies a promise of hiring.

At High Loft Accommodations, our employees face a seven-day orientation period.

When you start to work with High Loft Accommodations, you will begin by meeting someone from our HR Department and receiving our employee handbook. Your payroll information will be gathered and your benefits will be discussed in detail. You will also go through a series of training classes and an orientation meeting. You will then be placed with a supervisor who will show you the job for which you were hired.

At the end of the seven-day orientation period, you will have the opportunity to ask any questions regarding the handbook in a final training meeting.

At High Loft, we want you to like working with us. However, if you choose to leave your position, you are able to terminate employment with our company at any time for any reason because our employees are hired "at-will." We can also terminate the position at any time without giving notice or reason for our decision.

At the end of the orientation period, you will be considered trained for the position for which you were hired. However, you have no long-term guarantee of employment with High Loft Accommodations.

During the orientation or training period, most companies withhold company benefits, but if your company offers them, they could be mentioned in the statement above. You may also want to provide a clause in the above sample that states orientation may be extended up to another 60 days to make a better assessment of employment. By doing so, however, it is implied you intend to keep the employee so you will need to re-iterate the "at-will" clause.

HANDBOOK ACKNOWLEDGEMENT FORM

In the Appendix of this book and on the companion CD-ROM, you will find several generic sample forms for your handbook. You can use these forms as a template or basis to create your own forms with your own company information and needs. The handbook acknowledgement form appears first.

A copy of this form should be included in the handbook or given to the employee at the time of hire. The handbook acknowledgement form should be signed and placed in the employee file immediately upon receipt of the handbook, but the employee should be instructed to read the handbook and sign and return a copy of all the other forms required within a certain amount of time after being hired—a week is usually an appropriate time period to read and review the handbook and return all the forms.

In the future, there may be updates and changes to policies in the handbook, and later in this book we will talk about how to confirm that employees have received and added these updates to their copy of the employee handbook, but this form is the first and possibly the most important form to have on file to protect the company.

As the company owner or the CEO, you need to train the trainers and managers in your organization to make collecting these forms from new employees mandatory. You need to make sure they are also filed and copied. Remember, you must protect your company's interests.

NOTE ABOUT THE ACKNOWLEDGEMENT FORM

You will note that the acknowledgement form does not state that the employee has read the employee handbook. There are several reasons for this. First, it is important that the employee read and sign the employment "at will" policy information immediately, before they begin to interact with other employees and managers who may make inadvertent statements that an employee will misunderstand or could misconstrue as a contract or oral promise for continued employment if they have not already been informed otherwise.

Employees usually scan the handbook for items of immediate interest. For this reason, your handbook should be well organized and easy to search.

ELIGIBILITY

The federal Immigration Reform and Control Act mandates that all employers verify that each employee has a legal right to work in the United States within three days of employment. Verification of eligibility is simple. Your employees simply fill out an I–9 and show identification. This segment of the handbook will completely cover the identification process and eligibility. Your policy lets employees know they have to show proof of eligibility or they simply cannot work for you. Take a look at the handbook policy sample below:

Proof of Work Eligibility

Within three business days of your first day of work, you must complete Federal Form I-9 and show us documentation proving your identity and your eligibility to work in the United States. The federal government requires us to do this.

If you have worked for this company previously, you need only provide this information if it has been more than three years since you last completed an I-9 Form for us or if your current I-9 Form is no longer valid.

This section of the handbook will state who is in charge of the I–9 and verification process. Sometimes employers will begin their handbook with this particular section to be sure the employees working for the company understand they are required to provide proof of eligibility to work in the United States.

PERMANENT FILE

In the interest of employer/employee trust, it is important to let employees know the nature of material that will be kept in confidence in their employment file, including the location of the file and the fact that it is classified and under lock and key. Your policy may include the following information.

Your Personnel File Sample A

Containing the application for employment and references, these folders usually also bear records and information regarding compensation, payroll deductions, evaluations, and other information considered pertinent by (name of company).

Evaluations, correspondence, or other material received after initial employment making reference to an employee's competence or character shall not be placed in the personnel file of an individual without first requesting the employee to sign the document.

If the employee refuses to sign a document, it may be placed in the employee's personnel file if the employee's supervisor documents the employee's opportunity to sign, and a copy of the document, noting date of placement in the personnel file, is provided the employee. The employee shall also have an opportunity to attach comments.

Record of any grievance procedures shall be maintained separately from an employee's permanent personnel file. Each employee shall have the right to review the contents of his own file, with the exception of pre-employment reference recommendations.

Your Personnel File Sample B

This company maintains a personnel file on each employee to allow us to make decisions and take actions that are personally relevant to you, including notifying your family in case of an emergency, calculating income tax deductions and withholdings, and paying for appropriate insurance coverage.

Although we cannot list here all of the types of documents that we keep in your personnel file, examples include: _____.

We do not keep medical records or work eligibility forms in your personnel file. Those are kept separately. To find out more about those types of records, see Section ___ and Section ___, respectively, of this handbook.

Your personnel file is physically kept by _____.

If you have any questions about your personnel file,
contact _____.

AMERICANS WITH DISABILITIES ACT

Do you know what steps to take when an employee requests an accommodation for a disability? Responding correctly can mean the difference between defending against a discrimination claim and creating an effective working environment. It is necessary that your company respond to a request for accommodation, no matter how it may be worded. The Act applies to employers with 15 or more employees.

You have two major obligations under the *Americans with Disabilities Act* (ADA). First, you must not discriminate against qualified disabled individuals, and second, you must provide reasonable accommodations so that those qualified individuals can perform the essential functions of the job.

There are four basic principles that employers should apply to every accommodation decision:

1. The accommodation must be effective. In other words, it must provide an opportunity for the disabled person to achieve the same level of performance or enjoy equal benefits or privileges as an average, similarly situated, non-disabled person would.

2. The accommodation does not have to be the best accommodation or the one preferred by the disabled person.

3. The employer does not have to provide an accommodation that is primarily for the disabled individual's personal use such as a wheelchair or eyeglasses.

4. The ADA sets minimum guidelines for accommodation.

Whether you state your compliance with the Act in a formal policy is up to you, but you may wish to communicate your willingness to accommodate the disabled in your handbook.

SEXUAL HARASSMENT

Litigation against businesses makes it essential for most companies to adopt a policy against sexual harassment. It is important for personnel to know how to respond to a complaint of sexual harassment by conducting an investigation or in some instances hiring an attorney to conduct an investigation. Here is language that you may adapt for your company. Here is an example of a sexual harassment policy:

(Name of company) will not, under any circumstances, condone or tolerate conduct that may constitute sexual harassment by any of its employees. All our employees have the right to work in an environment free from any type of illegal discrimination, including sexual harassment. Any employee found to engage in such conduct will be subject to immediate discipline, up to and including discharge.

Sexual harassment is defined as:

Making submission to unwelcome sexual advances or requests for sexual favors a term or condition of employment.

Basing an employment decision on submission or rejection by an employee of unwelcome sexual advances, requests for sexual favors, or verbal or physical contact of a sexual nature.

Creating an intimidating, hostile, or offensive working environment or atmosphere either by verbal actions, including calling employees by terms of endearment; using vulgar, teasing, or demeaning language; or physical conduct which interferes with an employee's work performance.

We, at (name of company), do encourage healthy friendships among our employees; however, employees, especially management and supervisory employees, must be sensitive to acts of conduct which may be considered offensive by fellow employees and must refrain from engaging in such conduct.

It is also expressly prohibited for an employee to retaliate against employees who bring sexual harassment charges or assist in investigating charges.

Retaliation is a violation of this policy and may result in discipline, up to and including discharge. No employee will be discriminated against, or discharged, because of bringing or assisting in the investigation of a complaint of sexual harassment.

This policy does not address the investigation process that will be followed in the event of a complaint. Normally, this policy would be beyond the scope of the employee handbook. However, many of the losses incurred by companies in these cases were the result of reported complaints that the company did not act upon. Employers should follow through with the investigation process by providing formal training to personnel staff and supervisors when applicable. Letting employees know that this policy is in place may preclude its actually being tested in the workplace.

Shorter is almost always better. You may consider the following subjects for coverage in your handbook, and you may wish to deal with them simply. For ease of use, you may include an "Information at a Glance" section outlining your benefits packages. Include important phone numbers (such as group insurance numbers or the company code) and those phone numbers employees can use to speak directly with benefits representatives.

COMPANY OVERVIEW

Introduce your company with a few paragraphs about its history, growth, goals, ethics and management philosophy. We go into more detail later in this book.

EMPLOYEE "TO-DO" LIST

See the following sample.

Employee To-Do List
Please look this list over carefully. You are expected to take care of these items within your first few weeks of employment.
• **Identification card.** All employees and guests must carry a (name of company) ID card.
• **Paycheck.** You may choose either direct deposit or distribution through your department/division.

- **Employment status.** Know your employment status, payroll title, and personnel program, or collective bargaining unit.

- **Insurance plans.** You should enroll within (give deadline) of your hire date.

- **Parking.** Obtain a parking permit or inquire into commute options

- Equal opportunity statement

- State that an employee's religion, age, sex, or race will not influence hiring, promotion, pay, or benefits.

WORK HOURS

Define the work week and time allotted for lunch and breaks.

GENERAL INFORMATION

This section should be geared toward new hires who may not know the layout of the building, the time for lunch, or where to park. Consider including area maps, a parking pass, an organizational chart, phone lists, a statement regarding the confidential nature of your business, and policies addressing gifts, traffic tickets, personal telephone calls, and use of company cars.

PERFORMANCE AND PAY ISSUES

You may want to include a statement that written evaluations can occur at any time to advise workers of unsatisfactory performance. A statement about in-house as opposed to external hiring policies may also be appropriate under this subject. Pay issues should be treated with some delicacy. Therefore, avoid specific numbers or targets. Instead, include general statements about when paychecks will arrive, how promotions and wage increases are handled, classification of employees (exempt, nonexempt, part-time, full-time, on-call), policies on pay advances, leaves without pay, overtime, and exactly what areas they will be evaluated and how often. If you have no policy governing these matters, a policy to back up your handbook is imperative. Although the handbook is intended to avoid repetitive questions from employees, you should also add the department or name for the employee to contact with questions.

DISCIPLINE

Most employers follow some form of progressive discipline for performance problems or misconduct (attendance problems, difficulties getting along with coworkers, or missing deadlines, for example). You may choose to start with a verbal warning, followed by a written warning for a second offense, followed by a probationary period or suspension, then discharge for subsequent problems. Whatever system you implement, make sure to keep your options open.

Don't obligate yourself to follow a particular disciplinary pattern for every employee in every circumstance; otherwise, you may find it difficult to fire an employee for truly egregious behavior.

BENEFITS

List all the benefits and their restrictions for each class of employee and any restrictions that apply. Employees will be most interested in their direct costs for benefits. Ask your insurance company for their booklets that explain your insurance policies (such as health insurance, parental or maternity leave).

VACATION AND ALL TYPES OF LEAVE

Include all reasons for being absent from work, including: sick, military, bereavement, personal, family, medical, and jury duty. List paid holidays.

For simplicity do not lock yourself into differentiating between those employees who must work on holiday and those who do not. Merely include a statement that some employees may be required to work on holidays, and if there is a policy for overtime in place, you may provide it.

The usual practice in the United States is for employers to pay non-exempt employees time and a half for overtime. Some states take into account the toll that long-term overtime can take on employees and their families and the impact overtime work has on schooling and personal activities. Check the laws in your state before designing a back-up policy for overtime, and, again, allow your legal counsel to review all such policies and handbook statements for hidden promises of continued employment as well as implied promises of overtime pay.

PROFIT-SHARING PLANS OR PENSIONS

Discuss when and how employees become eligible for pension benefits, profit sharing, or contributions to their 401(k) plan. Employees will want to know whether their contribution is permitted or required, the amount the employer contributes, if any, and when employees become retirement vested.

Vesting is recognized as granting an eligible employee the right to specified pension benefits, regardless of discontinued employment status, usually after a fixed period of employment

SAFETY

State that employee safety is a major concern of your business and that employees are expected to follow safety rules and report any potentially dangerous conditions.

PROMOTIONS

Briefly stating your promotions policy will help to assure new and current employees alike that they will be treated fairly and that promotions take place from inside the company. (Otherwise, why would anyone stay with your company?) You may consider the following example for such language:

Promotions are based on qualifications and experience. Our policy is to fill vacancies by promotion from within with those candidates meeting or exceeding the qualifications whenever possible. Promotional opportunities are published in the job listing (state where) A promotion is defined as a change from a position in one classification to a position in another classification with a higher pay grade. Promotional increases vary and are coordinated through Human Resources (or state name of person). A transfer is a change from one position to another within the same classification title or pay grade assignment. It is a lateral change and involves no change in salary. Human Resources provides confidential job promotion and transfer counseling services for classified employees.

DISCHARGE

List the causes for which you will discharge an employee, including insubordination, criminal activity, dishonesty, poor performance, company policy violations, security breaches, absenteeism, and health and safety threats. You may present here, as in other areas, a disclaimer that the handbook is not a contract, policies can be changed at any time, and all employment is "at will."

FORMS

It is logical to have blank forms in the handbook in proximity to the subjects to which they refer. While individual businesses require various forms, consider including blank forms for time away from work, filing a grievance, travel reimbursements, performance reviews, pay advances, and accident reports.

BONUS STRUCTURE

The definition of a bonus is something given or paid over and above what is due. While it is not recommended that the percentage or amount of bonuses be listed in your handbook, it is recommended that you announce the fact that bonuses are awarded for work over and above what is due or for saving the company money through developing new step-saving processes. Your policy should state the reason for awarding a bonus with the caveat that a manager or owner may award a bonus at his or her discretion, if such is the case.

The importance of a notice in the handbook is to let employees know that bonuses are awarded to recognize certain accomplishments. You do not want employees finding out through the grapevine that some people received bonuses that were never announced. If the thinking is that employees are treated unfairly, the situation is almost impossible for management to overcome and usually leads to employees' seeking other employment. If your bonus system starts out being an incentive for diligence, it may backfire and become a reason for loss of workers—something that can usually be prevented by a simple announcement in your handbook that bonuses are awarded.

SUGGESTION BOX

If your company has a suggestion box for employees to drop in their money- and time-saving ideas, it is important that suggestions be publicized in the employee newsletter or on bulletin boards and answered in a timely manner. (Sometimes the answer has to be a polite "No.") Good suggestions that are implemented deserve a reward based on how much time or money they save. Get your new employees thinking about improving efficiency at your workplace on their first day by including an item in the handbook encouraging their suggestions, which can be signed or anonymous. Sometimes it is the fresh, new eye that sees the obvious that others miss on an everyday basis.

One more note on employee recognition. While cliques are certain to develop within any organization, try to keep recognition on the up-and-up rather than an occasion for certain people to be rewarded for being cute or having friends in high places. Such practices undermine any attempt on the part of management to show impartiality and fairness in the workplace and ultimately cause more problems than they are worth.

HAZARDOUS MATERIALS POLICY

If any of your employees come into contact with hazardous materials, it is necessary that one person, at least, be designated to collect information on such materials and post warnings for the safety of all. The policies under which this person conducts the hazardous material disposal depend entirely on state and federal laws. Your company should be in a position to assure all employees that every precaution is taken for their safety, in accordance with rules and regulations regarding each material.

VOTING AND POLITICAL PARTICIPATION

Your public election voting policy will be limited to allowing time for voting in cases where the employee cannot meet the polling deadlines because of distance, and whether you allow political campaigning, which is usually limited to the fact that you do not allow partisanship at the workplace nor do you allow after-hours campaigning (usually in the case of government employees). If you wish to address time off for voting, you may consider this notice for your handbook.

In most communities, polls remain open long enough to allow you time to vote without interruption of working hours. In cases of extreme hardship, such as great distance to the polls, you may be permitted to report to work late or leave early to vote. This time is given to you with pay and without reduction to your sick leave or annual leave, or any other leave benefit. If it is necessary for you to use this privilege, please notify your immediate supervisor before election day.

EDUCATION REIMBURSEMENT

If your company offers reimbursement for education, you will want to spell out how the employee qualifies, how much reimbursement the employee can expect, whether there is a limit to the number of courses one can take simultaneously, the grade requirement for reimbursement, whether courses must be work related, who grants approval of a proposed course of study, whether registration is permitted during working hours, whether work-time classes are allowed, and which schools are on a list for approved study. This is a benefit that attracts ambitious, hardworking employees and may be the one benefit that grooms employees for managerial positions.

REIMBURSEMENT FOR MOVING EXPENSES

Usually limited to executive or managerial positions, this benefit can take many forms in your policy manual such as the positions eligible and limitations of the benefit. Below is one possibility which you may wish to adapt for your policy and for your handbook.

Relocation Expenses

(Insert name of company) will pay for reasonable costs to relocate an applicant for (name of position) whose relocation is at the company's request and whose new, principal place of work is at least 50 miles further from the employee's home than his or her former job. Expenses will be reimbursed as follows:

- All moving expenses if the employee moves himself or herself. Packing materials will be paid for (boxes, tape, rental blankets, and dollies). Professional packing cost will not be paid. Contact (name of person) for assistance and to begin the process. He or she can obtain a discount with a self-move company.

- Half the moving expenses will be reimbursed if a professional moving company is used. Contact (name of person) for assistance and to begin the process. (Name of person) can obtain a discount with the moving company.

- Reimbursement for lodging up to three nights in a motel en route, if necessary.

- Mileage for one passenger car at the rate of (insert amount) cents per mile for the length of the move or reimbursement for your receipts.

Relocation Expenses Procedure

Approvals – Reimbursement of expenses depends on submittal of complete forms with accompanying receipts.

Income Tax Considerations – Some reimbursed relocation costs must be claimed as income. (Name of person) will provide the employee with a list of those items which are taxable for the employee's tax planning.

EMPLOYMENT OF MINORS

Any policy you develop to cover the occasional hiring of minors must comply with the federal Fair Labor Standards Act (FLSA). Furthermore, it is expected that you will require any supervisor who is considering hiring a minor to contact your HR department for approval. Whenever state law conflicts with FLSA, the more restrictive law applies. This is another area that your legal counsel should advise you about your company policy and keep you abreast of changes in the law.

A minor is considered anyone younger than 18. Minors who satisfy one of the following criteria are not subject to the FLSA:

- Have a high school diploma or a certificate of attendance or high school equivalent.

- Are heads of households or parents contributing to the support of children.

- Are employed by their parents in occupations not prohibited to minors.

- Are participating in a vocational program approved by the State Department of Education.

- Are employed delivering newspapers, mowing residential lawns, shoveling snow on a casual basis, acting or performing in motion pictures or theatrical productions or in radios or television productions, wreath making, and loading scrap balers or paper box compactors (if certain requirements are met).

All minors are prohibited from performing excavation work. Minors who are 14 and 15 are prohibited from occupations involving the operation of hoisting apparatus or power-driven machinery (including lawn mowers) other than office machines.

No one under 16 may be employed during school hours except as part of certain vocational programs. People under 16 may only be employed three hours a day and 18 hours a week when school is in session. They may be employed up to eight hours a day and 40 hours a week when school is not in session. During the school year, people under 16 may not work more than three hours in a day between the hours of 7 a.m. and 7 p.m. During vacations lasting five or more days and from June through August, people under 16 may work until 9 p.m.

Teenagers 16 and 17 years old are permitted more extended hours. They are prohibited from working:

- Before 7 a.m. Monday through Friday.

- Before 6 a.m. Saturday and Sunday in any week school is in session.

- After 11 p.m. on days before school days.

No minor may be employed for more than five consecutive hours without a rest period of at least 30 minutes. Minors are generally covered by the minimum wage laws applicable to adults. Overtime compensation should generally not be a concern since virtually all minors are prohibited from working more than 40 hours a week.

EMPLOYEE DISCOUNTS

Large companies are able to offer employees discounts with clients. If your company does so, it is important to let new employees know up front as discounts may make the difference in your company's obtaining a desired employee. Be sure to explain any limitations on the discounts and any requirements for obtaining them.

HIRING PROCESS

By the time employees have received a handbook, they have already been hired, right? So why have a section on hiring in the employee handbook? One reason is so that the newly hired employee can understand the process that his or her own resume and application went through before a position was offered, but it is also important in case a position opens within the company for which the employee, at a later date, may choose to apply. This can be a lateral move to a job more to their liking or a promotion to a position within the company for which they will have to submit an application just as any applicant would.

Another reason is that the employee may recruit other people from outside the company such as friends, family, and previous coworkers or supervisors for open positions within the company. It is important to spell out the hiring practices so everyone knows the company is fair.

Finally, communicating to the employees about the hiring process also helps to convey the culture, environment, and structure of the company especially pertaining to anti-discrimination and diversity issues.

EQUAL EMPLOYMENT OPPORTUNITY

Even though this statement is not required, and even though it is against the law to discriminate based on certain individual characteristics, it never hurts to reaffirm your company's commitment to Equal Employment Opportunity (EEO). When you have someone on your team who feels that at some point he or she was discriminated against, the EEO statement becomes important. Your company's statement can be as simple as the following:

Commitment to Equal Employment Opportunity

(Company name) believes all applicants and employees are entitled to equal employment opportunity.

At this point spell out exactly what characteristics you will not discriminate against, so that anyone working for or applying to the company understands that if they are in a protected status it is safe to apply to this company without fearing discrimination. You see this tag line, "We are an EEO employer" at the end of job search advertisements to let people know that the company is committed to equal employment to all. It can help during recruitment to attract a diverse applicant pool with strengths in key areas, while sharing a demographic comparable to the local area.

There are certain federally protected characteristics that must be included in your statement, and there are others that you may choose to include to define the culture and environment of your company's commitment to diversity.

Here are the Federal Laws Pertaining to EEO

Title VII of the Civil Rights Act of 1964 (Title VII) prohibits employment discrimination based on race, color, religion, sex, or national origin.

The Equal Pay Act of 1963 (EPA) protects men and women who perform substantially equal work in the same establishment from sex-based wage discrimination.

The Age Discrimination in Employment Act of 1967 (ADEA) protects individuals who are 40 years of age or older.

Title I and Title V of the Americans with Disabilities Act of 1990 (ADA) prohibit employment discrimination against qualified individuals with disabilities in the private sector and in state and local governments.

Sections 501 and 505 of the Rehabilitation Act of 1973 prohibit discrimination against qualified individuals with disabilities who work in the federal government.

The *Civil Rights Act of 1991* provides for monetary damages in cases of intentional employment discrimination.

(Source: EEOC Web site, **www.eeoc.gov**)

Some states have more stringent regulations than the federal government regarding the workplace and the hiring process. The following states have legislation relating to workforce discrimination based on sexual orientation: California, Delaware, Colorado, the District of Columbia, Illinois, Indiana, Maryland, Massachusetts, Michigan, Minnesota, Montana, Nevada, New Hampshire, New Jersey, New Mexico, New York, Oregon, Pennsylvania, Rhode Island, Vermont, Washington, and Wisconsin.

NOTE: This list was current at the time this guide was published, but it is important to note that antidiscrimination laws change regularly, so be sure to check the specific laws for your state before adding your policies in your handbook. An attorney should be able to provide language that will conform to your state's laws.

If you do not want to include a listing of the characteristics covered by your company's EEO policy, you would add the following sample text to the policy statement we have already mentioned:

Sample Additional Text

We follow all applicable local, state and federal laws prohibiting discrimination in hiring and employment. Our company does not discriminate against applicants or employees in violation of any of these laws.

If you have done your homework and know the specific laws that govern your area as far as EEO is concerned, you can include the following sample text in place of the text immediately above.

Sample Alternative Additional Text

Our company does not discriminate against applicants or employees on the basis of (Insert all characteristics that you want to include here), or any other characteristic or status protected by local, state, or federal laws.

RECRUITING

It is a good idea to have a current policy for recruiting and selecting employees. The methods to build an applicant base are important for you to know and to communicate to employees in case there is a desire to refer someone for an open position.

This policy will simply include the methods your company uses to recruit applicants. For example, if your company accepts applications and keeps them on file for future reference in case a position becomes available, it is important to let people know how long the application stays on file and whether they need to check back and ask to be considered for a position.

It is also a good idea to list places the company advertises open positions and how a candidate can apply after a position is posted. Some companies post only internally, some use their company Web site as the sole means of initial application, and some companies require that applicants apply in person. All means of application should be included in the recruiting policy for your company. We will start with a generic sample text to help you get a feel for how the policy should be worded.

> Our company can only be as good as the employees selected to represent us. Therefore we search all possible avenues to recruit talented and inspirational employees to fill our open positions. To achieve this diverse applicant pool we use the following methods to attract exceptional applicants:
>
> (List all methods used, such as newspaper advertisements, Web site listings, job boards, professional recruiting companies.)

Following this statement, you can specify any other programs that your company may use to recruit applicants. If you have a special relationship with a recruiting office or a staffing agency, include it here. More companies outsource some aspects of their business, finding that staffing agencies can handle a majority of their human resource needs in a more cost-effective manner. How you hire new employees would be appropriate for this section.

It is not easy to find the right people to fit the right job. "Diversity recruiting" is the current buzz phrase, and employers have become serious about hiring diverse employees. Some even offer bonus and referral programs for their current employees and contractors for bringing new applicants into the company for open positions.

If you want to encourage your current employees to refer applicants to open positions within the company, let them know by including that policy in your employee handbook. If you want to have a referral bonus program, you need to investigate the program so that it is fairly applied to all employees currently in your company.

After you have the referral program in place, you can let all the employees know about it by adding it to the employee handbook that they are required to read and understand.

Sample Text for Employee Referral Program

Our company encourages employees to recruit and refer applicants from the community for open positions within the company. If you refer an applicant who is hired and completes 90 days of employment with our company, we will provide a referral bonus to you.

Include specific information about your referral program here, including how to refer the applicant, and any reward due the referrer.

APPLICATION PROCEDURES

Application procedures vary between employers. Some employers do not have set application procedures but will find implementing one while creating the employee handbook is ideal. It makes the hiring process move at a faster pace.

INTERNAL APPLICATION PROCEDURES

If you wish to encourage employees to rise within your company, let your staff know that it is acceptable to apply for open positions, especially if it means a promotion. This is the place in the handbook to provide the process of applying.

Some companies give preference to applicants applying from within the company while other companies have decided that having a full applicant base both internally and externally is the best method for them.

Sample Optional Text for Internal Applicants
While we look outside the company for applicants for open positions, we also recognize the talents and experience of current employees who may wish to promote from within. We may post positions completely internally or that are available to both external and internal applicants.
We will post all internal job postings _____ (location of the internal job postings). If you are interested in applying for an open position, the company encourages you to apply by following our internal application procedures.
(Insert your step-by-step list of the internal procedures an employee should follow to apply for an open job posting.)

If you have input into the promotion policy at your company, remember that employees who move up within the company are happier and more productive staff members. If an employee has no room for change or improvement within the company, that employee may as well look for a job outside of the company. Hiring, training, and orienting an employee are expensive and time consuming. Promoting from within is a great way to retain experienced employees while allowing the employee develop their career

EXTERNAL APPLICATION PROCEDURES

Your company should determine how to handle the application process and create a policy for implementing the procedure. The policy should include where jobs are posted, how to apply for another position, and the follow-up internal process. When both of these—the internal and external application processes—are determined, you can then add them to the policy text of this section of your employee handbook.

EMPLOYING RELATIVES

Some employers have strict policies regarding family members' being employed concurrently. Some companies allow it but will not allow the employees to work in the same department or on the same shift. This policy needs to be addressed in your employee handbook so that there is no question about it. Whether to employ relatives can be a touchy subject, one that should be decided with the advice of an attorney or legal professional to ensure that your company does not violate any state or local laws.

There are few positive reasons for hiring family members to work for the same company. Nepotism is a breeding ground for legal and personal issues to wreak havoc on productivity.

Example: the owner of a company hires his 17-year-old son to work for the summer in the shipping and receiving department and tells the shipping manager to teach his son the ropes and treat him right. The son performs poorly on the job. How does the shipping manager handle this situation without jeopardizing his own job?

Many companies that conduct business in states and municipalities where it is legal to do so have a policy against hiring any relative. Some companies have a policy against hiring relatives only from the immediate, first-generation family, and others do not restrict hiring relatives, but limit related employees to working in separate departments or divisions, excluding any possibility of related employees' being in the other's chain of command.

Some states with stricter anti-discrimination statues and laws consider it discriminatory to refuse to hire someone or otherwise alter the employment status of an employee because that employee is related to or married to another staff member. These states allow civil and legal remedy should such discrimination occur. There are other states that deem nepotism regulations as an exception to the discrimination laws, and still others that have some type of legislation pertaining to nepotism that allows for exclusion under certain circumstances or situations only. This is why it is important to contact appropriate legal counsel to determine what the best policy is for your company, based on applicable laws for your company's location. The following are two sample policies for nepotism:

Policy 1: Nepotism Allowed Under Certain Circumstances

Employment of Relatives

As a general rule, there are no specific company policies excluding hiring relatives for most open job postings based solely on the fact that the applicant is related to a current employee. We encourage all applicants who are qualified for a position, regardless of their relation to a current employee, to apply for the position.

However, we do recognize that in certain situations, depending on the position and placement of the applicant and their relative, it may be inappropriate to hire a family member because of the possibility of negatively affecting the morale of other employees or creating a conflict of interest among the staff and relatives involved, particularly in the case where one relative would be supervising another. Because of this, we will not hire relatives of current employees for positions in which one family member would supervise another family member.

For the purposes of this policy, the term "relative" includes spouses, domestic partners, parents, children, siblings, in-laws, aunts, uncles, and cousins to include relations by blood/family, marriage, or step relations.

Policy 2 – Nepotism Not Allowed

Employment of Relatives

Our employees are valued members of our team, and we also value our employees' families. However, we have a policy against hiring family members of current employees for jobs within our company. For the purposes of this policy, the term "relative" will include spouses, domestic partners, parents, children, siblings, in-laws, aunts, uncles, and cousins to include relations by blood/family, marriage, or step relations.

Optional or Additional Policies

What should you do if two employees currently working for the company get married? If an exception is granted, it must be granted fairly to all persons involved. The company will definitely be put into a position of having to defend against discrimination accusations if one married couple is allowed to work for the company but another is not.

If the company strictly adheres to the policy of no relatives, one party in the marriage will be forced to resign or be discharged with cause. At that point, the company needs clear procedures on how to determine which employee should stay on and which should be discharged.

The company can choose seniority as a determining factor, allowing the employee who has worked for the company the longest to continue employment or perhaps rank within the company, meaning that the employee with the higher salary, high position in the chain of command, will stay on.

Either way the company decides there will be positives and negatives to either enforcing this policy or making an exception, and the company should weigh its options based on a clear-cut policy spelled out in the employee handbook. That is another reason to have an employee handbook—to communicate policies to employees beforehand, so that employees know exactly what to expect should this situation arise. In fact, your company can also include a policy about fraternization among employees in its handbook.

It is important that the employee handbook have clear, established policies pertaining to these issues so that the company can enforce its policies without exception.

DOMESTIC VIOLENCE POLICY

Few companies are progressive enough to address domestic violence in their work policies. If your company does, congratulations, because it entails offering help to an employee involved in domestic violence. If you plan to introduce such a policy, which is particularly recommended if you allow relatives to work for you, here is a sample definition from the public sector.

Domestic violence is defined as physical, emotional, sexual, or psychological abuse within a current or previous relationship, and/or family unit. The pattern of abuse can involve a wide range and combination of behaviors. It can take such forms as being kept short of money, being prevented from working, studying, or sleeping as well as physical abuse. Essentially it is about the misuse of power to assert and maintain control over another person.

The purpose of the policy itself can take this form:

We are committed to ensuring that any employee who experiences domestic violence can raise the issue at work and will receive appropriate support and assistance from us as their employer.

It is recognized that instances of domestic violence can have an impact on the workplace through lost productivity, absenteeism, and in some cases, threats and acts of domestic violence may actually carry over into the workplace. Therefore, the introduction of mechanisms and procedures to assist those experiencing domestic violence is an example of good management practice. Assisting and supporting individuals to resolve difficulties in their personal life will have a positive effect on their performance at work.

The aims of this policy are to assist and support employees who seek help in addressing problems arising from domestic violence; to ensure that these employees seeking assistance are responded to quickly, positively, and in confidence; and to assist and support managers in dealing with cases in a sensitive, fair, and consistent manner.

At this point you will want to provide a name within the company, usually the person who would handle sexual harassment complaints or a union representative, for an employee to report the need for help with assurance of confidence. That person should be made aware of new responsibilities in this area and given instructions for immediate follow-through. A part of your policy should contain this wording: "Disclosure of any information will only occur with the express consent of the employee."

The offer of employer help to an employee involved in domestic violence may take the form of paid time off for counselling, setting appointments with support agencies, and making arrangements for the care of the employee's children.

Should such violence occur at the workplace, it should be treated as any other case of harassment, with appropriate support (see above) for the employee or employees.

SECURITY

All employees should be provided a phone number to call in the case of an emergency. It may connect to your own security office or to the local police. Instructions for dialing need to include all numbers, if any, to reach an outside line.

If your company reserves the right to conduct searches of employees' desks and lockers, the handbook is the place to let employees know of this possibility as protection for the company. You may wish to incorporate language such as the following.

(Name of company) wishes to maintain a work environment free of drugs, alcohol, firearms, explosives, and other dangerous and problematic materials. To this end, we prohibit the control, possession, transfer, sale or use of such materials on its premises and require the cooperation of all employees in administering this policy. We reserve the right to conduct inspections to enforce this policy, and employees are required to cooperate with such inspections as a condition of continued employment. In enforcing this policy, we will endeavor to protect the privacy of individuals within the scope of the law.

SMOKING

If you provide an area where smokers can congregate to smoke, this is the place to let them know where it is and any other restrictions. As an incentive to stop smoking, your company may wish to institute a policy such as the following and notify employees through the handbook.

We provide reimbursement of up to $100 to employees who are smokers to participate in the smoking cessation program of their choice. Simply present a receipt, canceled check or insurance documentation to human resources to receive reimbursement. For those selecting the nicotine patch, the $100 reimbursement must be coordinated with our insurance coverage.

WEATHER

Here is a sample weather policy that you may wish to adapt for your employees and notify them by way of the handbook. This example is quite lenient and lengthy for ease in eliminating any parts that your company may find objectionable when creating its own policy

Weather Policy

In the event of severe weather, a decision on early dismissal or curtailment of services will be made by (name of person). After a decision has been made, supervisors will be notified by via e-mail and, if possible, by telephone about the details, including the official time of dismissal, if any. Individual departments may not release employees until they have received formal notification.

When faced with weather emergencies, we rely on managerial employees to handle their time wisely in completing work assignments. The additional responsibility and freedom allow employees, where appropriate, to take work home or to take limited amounts of time off during a regular working period. It is understood that employees ultimately must decide whether road conditions make their travel unsafe or unwise; that is, employees will not be asked to travel if they feel they are taking undue risk in doing so.

1. **Early Dismissal.** When inclement weather arrives during a workday, a decision may be made to dismiss employees early. Individual offices may not release employees until they have received formal notification of a company-wide decision. After that decision is made, supervisors will be informed via e-mail and, if possible, by telephone about the details, including the official time of dismissal.

   When a company decision has been made to dismiss early because of weather conditions, employees who are at work that day will be paid for their normal workday. Those who are required to stay beyond an official time of dismissal because of the nature of their work will be paid two times their normal earnings for the remainder of their normally scheduled hours. If an employee is required to stay beyond normal hours because of weather, the employee will receive two and one half times his or her normal earnings for those additional hours worked.

   Example: Employees are dismissed at 2 p.m. An employee who normally completes work at 4 p.m. is required to remain at her

Weather Policy Continued

post because of the nature of her work and receives two times her normal pay for the additional two hours. She is then asked to continue to work until 5 p.m., and is paid two and one half times normal pay for the additional hour.

2. **Late Arrival.** Inclement weather that occurs overnight may delay the timely arrival of employees. Employees who come to work under adverse weather conditions will be paid in full for that day, even though they may be delayed by the conditions and arrive late. Each employee ultimately must decide if road conditions make travel unsafe or unwise; that is, employees are not asked to travel if they feel they are taking undue risk in doing so. An employee who is unable to get to work because of weather-related conditions, even though the (name of company) is open, may use personal or vacation time as available, or elect to take the day without pay.

   Example: An overnight snowstorm makes travel extremely difficult during the morning rush hour. Employees who do not reach work at the time they normally begin work but arrive later in the day will be paid in full at their normal pay rate.

3. **Snow/Ice Day.** Work will be suspended only in extraordinarily difficult weather conditions. Only (name of person) may declare a snow/ice day. If at all possible, such a decision will be reached no later than 6 a.m. Employees will be notified of the snow/ice day via telephone or may call (phone number).

   All employees who were scheduled to work on a day that is declared a snow/ice day will be paid in full for the hours they were at work. An employee who does work on a snow/ice day will be paid two and one half times his or her normal earnings for all hours worked, regardless of his or her scheduled hours. Employees who are on a previously scheduled vacation or personal day will be paid vacation or personal pay as scheduled.

   Example: (Name of person) declares a snow/ice day. Most

Weather Policy Continued

employees are not asked to report but will receive pay as though they had worked a normal day. An employee reports to work. He arrives at 8 a.m., works his normal shift of eight hours, plus an additional two hours. He is paid two and one half times his normal rate for all ten hours he works on the snow/ice day.

RECYCLING

Your recycling policy can be a simple statement to let employees know that paper may be recycled into certain containers, giving their locations. If further recycling is available, mention that as well, such as containers for glass, aluminum, and cardboard. Consider encouraging recycling with this wording:

It is the responsibility of every employee to separate identified recyclable materials and place them in appropriate recycling containers. Office paper, corrugated cardboard, and aluminum beverage cans should always be recycled in the appropriately marked container. Other materials are to be recycled whenever feasible and wherever containers are provided.

Your policy may also include the use of recycled materials, in which case, you should inform employees as a gesture of public goodwill. Consider these points as part of your policy.

- Printing reports and documents, whenever possible, on both sides of the paper.

- Updating mailing and distribution lists periodically to avoid overrun; use of e-mail whenever appropriate.

- Giving preferential purchasing consideration to products that are reusable, refillable, repairable, more durable, less toxic, recyclable, and which avoid excess packaging.

5

EMPLOYEE CLASSIFICATIONS

Every employer must classify his or her employees so they can keep up with the various groups within the workplace. The way an employee is classified often determines salary, benefits, vacation time. The main employee classifications are as follows:

- Temporary

- Part-time and Full-time

- Exempt and Nonexempt employees

An employee may have more than one classification. For example, the temporary employee could be considered a temp working part-time. The important thing is you have a way to classify your employees so that they are aware of the benefits due them.

TEMPORARY EMPLOYEES

Even if you prefer to have fully dedicated employees who work all the time for you, it may become necessary to employ temporary employees who will work for you at a designated time of the year or through a particular increase in productivity. Regardless of whether you employ temps through an agency or on your own, they need to know they are indeed, a temporary employee and kept under the umbrella of the temporary classification. Take a look at a sample policy you can use for your temporary employees:

Temporary Employees

Sometimes at KDJ Trucking, we hire temporary office employees for a busy season. The following policy is enforced and not implied.

The individuals we hire for a temporary position are referred to as "temporary employees." They do not receive benefits and are not to refer to themselves as employees of the company. They are not eligible for paid time off or for sick leave.

Temporary employees work for KDJ Trucking "at will" meaning they can be discharged at any time without notice. At the same time, they can terminate their employment with KDJ Trucking at any time without notice.

If a temporary employee is offered employment with KDJ Trucking, they will go through the formal hiring process and may receive a written offer to join the company through a full-time or part-time position which would also be a position with the company "at-will."

Please sign below if you understand the temporary policy.

Employee Signature: _____

Employee Printed Name: _____

A temporary policy can be simple and straight to the point and should include the "at-will" clause.

FULL-TIME AND PART-TIME EMPLOYEES

You need to determine what will constitute full-time and what will constitute part-time employment with your company. Some companies go by the 40-hour mark. Anything 40 hours and above constitutes a full-time employee. Some consider an employee full-time if he or she works over 30 or 34 hours per week. Whatever your mark is, you need to relay this to the employees who work for you in written format just in case there is ever any question. Take a look at a good policy sample:

Part-time and Full-time Employee Classification: At Pete's Wholesale, the number of hours you work per week determines your benefits as an employee of our company. You must be considered a part-time or a full-time employee and understand certain benefits apply to each.

Full-time Employees: If you are an employee who works your regular schedule in the amount of 36 hours or more per week, you are considered a full-time employee of Pete's Wholesale.

Part-time Employees: If you are an employee who works your part-time schedule of less than 36 hours per week, you are considered a part-time employee.

An employee may switch back and forth between full- and part-time schedules with some ulterior motive such as getting benefits. For this reason, the best policy on vacation time is so many hours earned for hours worked rather than simply by classification.

NONEXEMPT AND EXEMPT EMPLOYEES

The "nonexempt" and "exempt" employees are a classification that refers to whether the employee is paid overtime. See the following for a sample policy.

Whether you receive overtime pay depends on your status as either an exempt or nonexempt employee. Nonexempt employees are covered by overtime under the Fair Labor Standards Act. Exempt employees do not earn overtime. They fall under the right provisions for the Fair Labor Standards Act and do not qualify for overtime pay. If you have questions about the exempt and nonexempt employee status, please let us know.

If not, please sign below stating you fully understand this policy and indicate in writing your employee classification.

Employee Signature: _____

Employee Printed Name: _____

In most cases, a salaried employee is an exempt employee and the employee typically understands he or she does not earn overtime. If you have questions about the classifications, consult the Fair Labor Standards Act for more information.

JOB SHARING

If your company relies on job sharing to fill certain positions, the company policy should spell out whether the persons sharing a job must take responsibility for the work in the absence of the other person and whether one job sharer is responsible to find a replacement should the other leave the company. If so, to convey this information to employees, consider this language.

A job-sharing team is made up of no more than two persons who are employed in one full-time position. The team shares full responsibility for the job, and if one member of the team cannot cover his or her hours, the other member is expected to step in.

A team may be created to fill an open position within a department or to accommodate a valued employee who wishes to work fewer hours. In this case, the supervisor will determine if job sharing is an appropriate alternative, and the employee is expected to find the other member of the team. Job sharers will receive a detailed set of guidelines and will be expected to sign a job sharing agreement at the beginning of employment.

The following are some of the policies that apply to a job-sharing team:

Resignation/discharge – If a member of a job-sharing team resigns or is discharged, the other member must either assume full-time responsibilities or identify a new job sharer, subject to the supervisor's approval, within 30 days of the resignation or discharge. If the remaining job sharer either cannot work full-time or find a replacement, she or he will be discharged because of an inability to meet the position's hours requirement.

Reduction in force – If the position shared by the team is subject to a reduction in force, both members would be covered by the terms of the (name of company's) reduction-in-force policy. If the severance benefit applies, each job sharer will receive a pro-rated portion of the severance pay he or she would have earned if full-time.

Of course, if one job sharer does not bear these responsibilities, substitute the name of the person (presumably in HR) who does.

Flex Time

The following policy may be adapted and included in your handbook.

Flex Time

An employee may establish a 40-hour work week or a time schedule that differs from the regular daily schedule if the needs of both the individual and the (name of company) are served. Such an agreement must be in writing, signed by (name of person) and the employee. A copy is sent to (name of person or department) and is included in the employee's file.

6

WORKING HOURS

ABOUT WORK HOURS

You want to list your normal operating hours in your handbook. If you are open around the clock, you want to list you are a 24-hour operating facility. If you have set or pre-determined hours, you should include this as well. Take a look at one sample you can use in your own handbook to describe policies of working hours.

Hours of Operation
JB Enterprises operates from 9 a.m. until 9 p.m. Monday through Saturday.

Some companies prefer more than a simple statement about working hours. Take a look:

Hours of Operation
JB Enterprises operates from 9 a.m. until 9 p.m. Monday through Saturday. We do not offer or expect overtime after 9 p.m. Your shift ends promptly at that time. We ask that all vehicles be removed from the premises at 9 p.m. and inform all employees that the gate is locked at 9:30 p.m. and re-opened at 8 a.m. Thank you for your cooperation.

When addressing the hours of operation, you should list any extenuating circumstances about the hours of operation or the building's access before or after hours of operation.

In the hours-of-operation provisions, you may mention the specific hours an employee will be required to work as it pertains to scheduling, such as, "Your team leader will hand out work schedules at the end of each month. These schedules will list your start and finish time on each day of the week."

If you run a company that operates on a 24-hour rotating shift schedule, you may wish to alter the schedule further. Take a look:

The Letter Company operates 24 hours. Our shifts run from 2 a.m. to 10 a.m., 10 a.m. to 6 p.m., and 6 p.m. to 2 a.m. seven days a week. You will have a designated shift assignment unless you work in Production One where you will have swing shift rotations.

If you need to change shifts, please talk to the HR Department. Every effort will be made to accommodate your needs. However, we do not guarantee changes in shifts.

You are welcome to change shifts with another person from time to time. More than three shift changes in any calendar month will be cause for dismissal.

FLEXTIME

Many companies have begun to offer flexible scheduling to allow employees more time with their growing families or to enjoy activities outside of work. The following policy covers flextime for your handbook.

Flextime Scheduling

We know it is important to juggle home and work in a way to enjoy both. We have decided to offer our employees a plan for working more flexibly. If you want to work on a flextime schedule, please see someone in HR. The company welcomes the opportunity to be accommodating on flextime scheduling if at all possible. We never guarantee we can accommodate your flextime request but we will try to meet your needs as well as the needs of the company.

If you cannot be fair in your flextime scheduling, then you should not offer it. You can open the door to discrimination charges if you do not divide the flextime schedules equally.

BREAKS

Employees are offered a certain amount of breaks during the workday. Some states even mandate paid breaks while the employee is on the time clock. You should know what kind of breaks you intend to offer across the board and list the information about these breaks in the handbook. You may want to mention whether your company requires employees to clock in and out for breaks and lunches, an advantage to the employer who wants to know precisely how to calculate employees' paychecks. Employees should know whether breaks are paid, how often they occur, and where they are to be spent. Here is a sample:

Regarding Meal Breaks and Other Short Breaks

Employees are permitted to take one 15-minute break for every four hours worked. These breaks are not paid breaks so you must clock in and out and you must take your breaks. Your meal break is not paid, and you are required to clock in and clock out for meal breaks as well. You are allotted a 30–minute meal break. You may not skip your lunch break and take off work 30 minutes early unless approved by a supervisor at least 24 hours in advance.

Paid or unpaid, breaks should be well defined in the handbook so there are never any questions about them.

OVERTIME

If you know you may have employees who will be required to work overtime occasionally or even on a consistent basis, you should adopt a policy to include in your handbook. The overtime policy should be directed toward your entire work force and not just one or two departments, if at all possible. Even if you only have one or two departments that work overtime, try to keep everything general to avoid charges of discrimination. Take a look at the following sample:

Overtime

Occasionally, you may be asked to work overtime. While overtime is not always mandatory, it is occasionally requested and one of the conditions of employment is that we expect our employees to take several overtime shifts during each calendar month.

We try to give some notice but on occasion, doing so is impossible. If we have enough volunteers for overtime, we do not need to mandate overtime work hours.

Conditions of overtime vary from nonexempt employees to exempt employees. See your supervisor if you have questions in regard to your classification and the provisions for overtime. Keep in mind, all overtime must be approved by a supervisor. Working overtime without the consent of a supervisor or team leader is cause for question.

Nonexempt employees receive 1.5 times their standard rate of pay when working overtime.

Sometimes employees desire overtime work, and other times it may be difficult to find volunteers for overtime. If you know you have a difficult time finding volunteers for overtime and often need it, make sure you include the policy you want to follow in your handbook. Take a look at this sample:

Overtime Policy

We occasionally have overtime available for those who would like to work overtime. Each day when you clock in, take a moment to look over the overtime opportunities posted. If you know you can work an overtime shift, please sign up for it. If not, we will begin a rotating schedule mandating overtime. The overtime at this company is limited but does exist. It is a condition of employment, and employees should expect some overtime shifts.

In California, if overtime is worked, it is paid at the rate of double time rather than time and a half. Overtime rules and regulations will vary by states requiring you to be knowledgeable about your state's requirements

Employers need to convey every little detail about overtime and regular salary requirements in the handbook. Take a look at the following:

Vacation time, holidays, and any other PTO time used do not count as time actually worked when calculating overtime. The hours actually worked at the company on the clock must pass the 40–hour mark to be considered for overtime.

Some employers will count the paid time off as hours worked. While doing so can cost the company an excessive amount of money paid out in salaries, it is a matter of choice. If you choose to allow employees to count their paid-time-off hours toward actual worked hours in any work week, you may want to incorporate the following policy into your handbook:

Vacation time, holidays, and any other PTO time used do count as time actually worked when calculating overtime. After the total hours worked and the PTO time exceeds 40 hours, the employee will qualify for overtime.

You may want to add another provision in your handbook regarding volunteering for overtime.

WHERE TO FIND MORE INFORMATION

Most states have laws and implementation regulations regarding meal breaks, other breaks, and overtime. Obtain all pertinent laws from your state department of labor or consult a labor-relations attorney to help you with accurate language for your employee handbook.

Pay specifics are a crucial part of your handbook. Employees like to understand all of the pay policies and they want to feel good about them. They want to know how and when they will be paid. They want to know they are receiving all the information they need to make their time on the clock worthwhile. The pay area of your handbook should cover this area sufficiently to ensure that your employees understand the policies of your company regarding their payment.

This chapter concerns pay policy information for your employees. You will be able to convey to them what you need them to know about employee pay in general including how to get extra pay incentives as well as what they need to know about withholding and other deductions that affect their income.

THE PAYCHECK

No one works for free. The fact is no one would work for the other guy if they could get around it. Part of the American dream is to work for yourself, yet millions of Americans work for someone else. They punch a clock day in and day out so they expect to be compensated for it and hope to be content with that compensation. Your employees may like you but not well enough to show up for free. You need to let them know in your handbook when they can expect their paycheck. It's a good idea to include a mock check illustrating typical deductions and other information since every company's checks are unique.

Before making provisions for this policy in your handbook, check with the U.S. Department of Labor for the law pertaining to payment frequency. Find out the law before you begin to incorporate the pay policy into your handbook. Consider the following sample policy.

> **Payday**
>
> Our employees are paid the first and third Fridays of every month. You will receive your paycheck at the end of your shift on Friday or you may stop by and pick it up after 11 a.m. if you are not scheduled to work that particular day. If payday falls on a holiday when the business is closed, you may pick up your paycheck at the end of the business day before the holiday.

Most employers will pay before the holiday to ensure they stay within the requirements of their state.

TIME SHEETS

Regardless of whether your employees keep time sheets with a written record of the hours they have worked or they clock in and clock out on a time card, it is important to implement a policy regarding how the information gets to the payroll department. Let your employees know what you expect and the best procedure to follow to ensure they are paid in a timely manner. Take a look at this suggested policy you may wish to incorporate into your manual.

> Employees should sign their time cards and turn them into HR at the end of their last shift at the end of their work week—either Friday or Saturday.

Of course you want to prevent employee theft of company time by controlling access to time cards by other employees who may clock in or out for a friend who is not actually working. Let employees know in the handbook that there is a penalty for such action (usually dismissal) with a reminder that supervisors are expected to know who is present and to approve time cards.

ADVANCES

Whatever policy you adapt on payroll advances should be kept uniform. If you allow one employee to get an advance, you must allow any employee to obtain an advance. The best policy to have is not to allow advances, but it is a matter of choice. A word of caution: you will open yourself up to endless problems if you begin to offer advances to employees who ask for them. Fortunately for the employer, advancing money to employees is not a requirement by law. Still, you should adopt a policy to follow and stand by it so you can save yourself aggravation later. You should handle the policy regarding advances with kid gloves. Take a look at the following suggestions you may want to incorporate into your handbook:

Our Policy Regarding Advances

Our company chooses not to allow advances to employees. We do not advance anyone any amount on their paycheck regardless of the reason. We understand that from time to time, situations place a family in need of extra income. If such a situation arises, please talk to your supervisor and we will do what we can to accommodate your need by allowing you as much overtime as possible whenever the company has available shifts for overtime.

Here is a simple policy statement:

We do not offer advances. We never offer or allow advances to any employee.

Often if you keep things simple, you shut the door to possible questions about the policy you have in effect. If your company allows advances, there should be limits. Take a look at the suggested sample below.

Our Policy Regarding Advances

JB Trucking allows paycheck advances for employees who have been with us for more than 90 days. However, these advances are limited to 50 percent of your net pay per pay period and will be at the discretion of the HR Department. We limit our employees to fewer than six advances a year. If you are in need of overtime, please see your supervisor.

A pay policy needs to explain how much pay can be advanced on the pay period. Is it a set amount or a percentage of the individual's paycheck? The policy should set the repayment plan of the advance and finally, it should stipulate who makes the decision regarding an advance.

When you discuss the handbook with your employees, take pains to mention your take on advances. Make sure your employees know your company is not in the banking business (even if it is a bank!) and does not like to offer advances but will in certain circumstances.

REPAYMENT OF THE ADVANCE

If you are going to offer advances, you should let the employees you have working for you know how they will be expected to repay these. The best way to do this is to have the entire amount taken out of the next paycheck. However, this is not always practical. Take a look at the following samples and see which one you think will work for you.

Repaying Your Advance

Should you choose to take an advance against your paycheck, it must be repaid within 30 days of the time you receive it. If you have an unpaid advance and you request another advance, you may be turned down.

The problem with advances really is two-fold. You allow your employee to depend on you whenever they cannot make ends meet, and you allow the employee the opportunity to sink further behind in their bills by offering them a quick-fix to their money flow issues.

Repaying Your Advance

Through the payroll department, your advance will be paid back within four weeks. The amount you are advanced will be taken out of your paycheck in four equal payments to ensure your advance is paid back in a timely fashion.

You should check with your state regarding advance terms to ensure you are following your state's laws and guidelines. NEVER pay an advance in cash or through petty cash. Always use a standard payroll procedure when paying an advance, taking care to note any deductions and the number of hours to be worked to cover the fee advanced.

If you are going to advance your employees money from time to time, you should use a payroll deduction authorization form. It can be basic like the form below:

On _____, I requested a payroll advance from Galloway Shoes. The advance is treated as a loan from my employer. I agree to repay this loan by four payroll deductions of _____ to cover the entire amount advanced.

If my "at-will" employment is discharged before the advance is repaid, my last payroll check will reflect the entire amount withheld to satisfy the debt.

Signed_____

Witnessed _____

Total Amount Advanced _____

VACATION AND HOLIDAYS

Some employers will allow employees to obtain their paycheck early if they are going on vacation and will be away during the pay period. If you are going to do this, you need to be fair about it and allow it for everyone. If you think you are going to run into a problem with it, do not do it. Paying your employees whenever they ask to be paid can create numerous problems you do not need.

You should add another clause to your handbook if you are going to allow your employees to be paid before a vacation. Take a look:

If you are going on vacation and do not want to ask for an advance beforehand but will be away when paychecks are disbursed, you may request your paycheck three days before the start of your vacation. Each employee is allowed one early disbursement per calendar year.

If you do not want to offer the employee a paycheck early, you may want to place a different type of stipulation.

If a pay period falls while you will be on your scheduled vacation, please allow the HR Department to take care of your payroll needs. Let someone in HR know if you would like to have your check mailed to your home or held until your return from vacation.

If you present options to your employees in a positive light, you will be able to give the employee a choice that will sound so appealing that he or she will hesitate to ask for a paycheck early. Offer to help them out by sending their check to their home so they will not have to interrupt their vacation in anticipation of payday. If they are out of town, they may appreciate arriving to a check in the mail.

SHIFT DIFFERENTIALS OR PREMIUMS

In some positions with certain employers, a shift differential is common practice. In many cases, any shift other than day shift will warrant the employee's getting paid a little more on the hour. You should discuss any difference in pay in your handbook so you can allow employees to know their fellow employees are paid more for doing the same job because of working on a shift premium. The following is an example of what you may want to use.

Shift premiums are paid for each shift after 5 p.m. Our second shift premium will be 50 cents and our third shift premium will be $1. For example, if you typically earn $9 per hour for day shift, you would earn $9.50 per hour on second shift and $10 per hour on third shift.

In some states, a shift premium is also granted for split shifts. The labor department in your state can answer any questions you have about shift premiums.

TIPPING

You may want to include in your handbook an area about tipping. If you are in the food service industry or in any industry where tipping is customary, you want to advise your employees of your tipping policy. You will especially want to address the issue of how tipping can change the standard wage requirements as mandated by the laws of your state.

Tipping
Our customers tip generously for good service. If you are an employee who is able to share in tips from the customers, you will receive your tips plus an hourly wage that is less than the minimum wage. However, if your tips do not add up to the minimum wage per hour, you will be paid the difference.

You need to discuss tipping and "tip-outs" in your handbook. A tip-out occurs when an employee working for tips is required to pay part of the tips to the bus boy or bartender, for instance. In hair salons, a beautician will often tip-out to the receptionist or the person responsible for shampooing clients before the beautician sees the client. If you require tip-outs to other employees, you need to advise your employees how they should tip out and when. Take a look:

Tipping-Out
If you hold the position of _____, you are required to tip out to the following positions_____ _____. We require 10 percent of your tips to be pooled with the other employees to ensure everyone goes home at the end of their shift with tips. If you have questions, see the manager on duty.

You can run into problems with tipping out. You should know what the law states before you begin to require tipping-out from your employees.

There are some stipulations to the tipping-out policies that vary by state. You can never expect employees to tip out so much that they take home less than the minimum wage per hour. They should only be expected to contribute fairly and only if all employees of the same title are tipping-out to these positions as well. Before writing your section on tipping, check your state's laws. By law tips are never the employer's to keep.

DEDUCTIONS

Deductions should be clearly defined. Whenever an employee has deductions coming out of his or her check, the person will want to know how much was deducted and why. Deductions include, but are not limited to, flexible spending accounts, insurance, union dues, charity, contributions to savings or 401K accounts, and other deductions authorized by the employee. You may cover your policy on payroll deductions as follows:

Payroll Deductions
You will have mandatory deductions withheld from your paycheck as required by law. These deductions include FICA and withholding for state or federal income tax. However, you can initiate deductions for flexible spending, savings, charity and other reasons. Please contact Shirley in payroll for more information.

ANY REIMBURSEMENTS

If you know there will be times when you need to reimburse your employees, you need to choose how you will do this and include in your handbook the appropriate steps your employees should take when requesting a reimbursement. Take a look at the following suggestion.

Expense Reimbursement

Occasionally, you will need to be reimbursed by (name of company). Please follow this procedure to be reimbursed promptly. Failure to follow these guidelines for reimbursement can result in delayed repayment.

- Check with a supervisor to ensure you will be reimbursed for your expenses.

- Spend your money conservatively and use the recommended merchants for your purchases or overnight travel and lodging.

- Keep your receipts; you will need them for any reimbursement.

- You must submit your receipts within 45 days of the date on the receipt to be reimbursed for any material, meals, or lodging.

- You will need to obtain an expense report and fill it out completely with your supervisor.

- You will receive approved reimbursements within ten days of submitting your report.

Some states have laws about items employers require their employees to buy. If you are unsure of your state's requirements, you should check with the department of labor in your state to ensure you handle this policy correctly.

If you are going to require an employee to use particular merchants or vendors, you would want to add a simple statement like this sample:

Since our company is owned by the CTL Group, we only reimburse from the following CTL merchants:

CTL Restaurants including Tucker's Tavern, Irish Burger, The Greek Spoon, China Garden by CTL, and Caravan's. We also reimburse from any CTL owned hotel. For a complete list, please see the HR Department.

All material and tools should be purchased through the CTL group of approved vendors which is subject to change. You may obtain this list through the HR Department as well.

In the case of a list of vendors and merchants, you may want to keep this in the HR Department so that no alterations can be made to it. Occasionally, vendors and merchants will offer kick-backs to large companies who trade with them and it is important that the person in charge choose such businesses.

DETAILED TRAVEL REIMBURSEMENTS

If your company requires employees to travel from time to time or on a consistent basis, you will need a procedure for recording expenses the individual will incur. Travel expenses need to be well organized in a document given to payroll or the HR Department. The sample below can be used for the traveling sales representatives or other employees who will need to travel as part of their job description:

Procedures for Reimbursement for Travel

GH Foods will reimburse you for the following when you are traveling on behalf of our company:

- All costs incurred traveling to and from the airport and all parking expenses.

- All costs for traveling by other means.

- Costs incurred for hotel stays.

- The cost of meals and other expenses up to _____ per day.

- If you use a car for your travel and it is NOT a company car, you will be paid 30 cents per mile.

GH Foods has a standard policy in effect for reimbursements. You will not be able to have your expenses reimbursed if you do not have a supervisor's signature on the final record of expenses. You will document all expenses and include your receipts with the report before turning it into the HR Department for final approval. All reimbursements will be paid within 10 days.

If you choose to reimburse for mileage, you may want to list a separate procedure for your employees to follow. Many companies have their employees simply keep a log of their mileage. The following samples are examples of wording you may need.

MILEAGE REIMBURSEMENT

When choosing to reimburse our employees for mileage, we make sure we pay you in a timely manner but must stipulate accurate logs of your mileage. We supply gas and mileage logs for our representatives. Please see the HR Department for a new log before traveling.

If you are not going to use a log book, consider this form:

Mileage Reimbursement
You will be reimbursed for your for gas, mileage, and vehicle maintenance for as long as you are classified as an outside sales representative with our company. The following are guidelines for reimbursement: • Keep a journal of your travel, logging destination, mileage, and date. Include name of business and person you saw.   • Always have your supervisor's written approval before you travel.   • Turn in your record every Thursday for approval from payroll.   • Your reimbursements will be paid on the following Monday.

FURTHER DETAILS OF YOUR REIMBURSEMENTS

Reimbursements should be at the discretion of the supervisors and HR Department. If you do not want to pay for travel that is not work-related, keep a close eye on your new and seasoned sales representatives alike. Otherwise, your company may end up paying for car repairs, gasoline, and maintenance.

Make sure you stipulate which job titles will be eligible for certain reimbursements. For instance, in the previous example, you will note the employee will know certain reimbursements apply as long as he or she remains an outside sales representative (or other traveler for the company).

Using expense forms can be advantageous to the company. Some companies use envelopes for the employee to place receipts in and record pertinent information on the back of the envelope. With the handbook, you should be able to note your procedure and include your standard forms in the back of your handbook.

Below is a sample reimbursement form for your use as a model to devise one for your company. You can come up with an expense record more tailor-made to your company or you can also find one at an office supply store. Still, you should include a sample in your handbook so your employee will know what to expect. Place it with your procedure for reimbursements. Your employees need to know what to do and you need to make things easier for the person who processes these expenses. Presenting it in the handbook is crucial.

| Expenses for _____ |
| Pay Period Ending the week of _____ |

Date on	Purchased Item	Reason
Enclosed Receipt	or Service	Cost
Reimbursed		
1., (2 and so on)		

Employee's Signature _____

Manager's Signature_____

Date Approved by Payroll _____

Signed_____

If you make your standard policy widely known it will be accepted, making reimbursement a simple procedure.

7

EMPLOYEE BENEFITS AND USE OF COMPANY PROPERTY

A "must" for any handbook is employee benefits. Changes in benefits such as providers can be incorporated into the handbook at any time if you are well prepared from the start ensuring you cover the key points of the employee benefits you offer.

It is estimated that anywhere from 30 percent to 40 percent of an employee's compensation is realized through benefits. It is your job to make sure your employees recognize the benefits your company is providing to them and their families.

Naturally, you should cover your benefits with the employee during the orientation and ideally, you will not simply hand them the handbook and tell them to read all about the benefits you offer. Your employee will remember more about the benefits package you offer them if you first tell them and then provide them with the written information for future reference.

THE BENEFITS

Ideally benefits are covered during orientation. After that, you should be able to describe the benefit plan briefly in the handbook as the following notice shows.

Welcome to (Name of Company)
Our Company Benefits
As part of our commitment to become one of the best companies in this state, we offer our employees the following benefits packages: Include every option you offer from PTO to stock options.)
We are happy to provide you with a full benefits package. If you have any questions about the plan we offer, please contact Kathy in Human Resources.

Keeping the introduction to company benefits simple is a good way to let your employees know what to find in the benefits section. The following benefits should be covered in this area of the handbook:

- Overview of benefits

- Insurance coverage for the employee's specific family members

- Health care benefits for the employee

- Disability

- Worker's compensation

- Unemployment

- 401(k) and Stock Options

- PTO (paid time off)

- Retirement benefits

You will be able to incorporate each of the above into a small section of your handbook. You should decide if you want to discuss each of the above entities separately within the handbook or jointly and then by directing the employee through the proper channels to receive more information. You may simply want a statement in your handbook like this:

More about Your Benefits

Should you wish to find out more about your employee benefits, you may contact the HR Department. You will receive a benefits package from the HR Department during orientation, and all of your benefits will be explained to you completely. However, if you have further questions, please contact Kathy in our HR Department for further information.

It is important to tell your employees where they can go for more information while taking care to hit the high points of the benefits your employees will receive.

You may wish to define "401(k)" in the handbook and let employees know when they may opt in and the percentage the company will contribute. Following is a definition which you may adapt for your use.

A 401(k) plan is a type of employer-sponsored *retirement plan* named after a section of the United States *Internal Revenue Code*. A 401(k) plan allows a worker to save for retirement while deferring *income taxes* on the saved money or earnings until withdrawal. The *employee* elects to have a portion of his or her *wage* paid directly, or "deferred", into his or her 401(k) account. In participant-directed plans (the most common option), the employee can select from a number of investment options, usually an assortment of *mutual funds* that emphasize *stocks, bonds, money market* investments, or some mix of the above. Many companies' 401(k) plans also offer the option to purchase the company's stock. The employee can generally re-allocate money among these investment choices at any time. In the less common trustee-directed 401(k) plans, the employer appoints trustees who decide how the plan's assets will be invested.

Do not allow your language to promise this benefit, which is out of the hands of your company. For information on Worker's Compensation go to **www.workerscompensation.com**.

USING THE COMPANY "STUFF"

If you own a large company or you are the "go-to" person, you know everything in the company belongs to you either directly or indirectly. You are ultimately responsible for the day-to-day operations, employees, profits, and the assets such as cars, forklifts, and furniture.

The best way to watch the company assets can be to have policy details in your handbook. Since most of the benefits mentioned earlier in this chapter will be covered under another set of documents and folders, this is a policy you will want to describe thoroughly so your employees will be able to understand the way you want them to take care of company property. The following is an example of company policy for maintaining company cars.

Company Cars

You must have a license to drive if you are going to drive one of our company cars, and a copy of your license must be on file in the HR Department. When you are out in the field we expect you to drive one of our cars. We request that you record mileage on the sheets located in the glove box of the car. Please take a moment to note your trip in the log at the end of the day for our technicians' use.

We expect the car that is provided for your use to be kept in working order meaning that we want fuel in it when you return from your outside duties of the day. Please remove all items from the car and keep it as clean as possible so the next driver will be glad to drive one of our company cars with his clients as well.

You may use our cars only for business purposes. Do not drive with family members in the car and do not run personal errands while you are on the clock. If we discover you have abused the car in any way or have driven one of our cars under the influence of drugs or alcohol, your employment will be discharged immediately.

You can alter any of these policy samples and examples in this handbook but sticking with the main principle will help you write a more effective handbook. Take a look at the policy regarding telephones:

The Policy of Phone Calls and Our Telephones

Our phones are for business purposes only. If you need to make a personal call, do so on your breaks, using the phones located _____. We also have pay phones throughout the plant for your use, or you may use your cell phone in the outside courtyards. Thank you for your compliance with this rule. It is for the benefit of all staff.

You may not want your employees to tie up your company phone. It is best to implement the "no-call" rule; otherwise, someone will always be on the phone calling home or placing calls to loved ones.

Another company policy you need to cover in your handbook is the return of all company property upon discharge. You should not only mention this in orientation but you need to incorporate it into your handbook for all employees to review as needed. You can keep this section of the handbook simple and straightforward.

At the end of your association with our company, we expect all of our training materials, employee handbooks, manuals, and other company items to be returned to Stan in the HR department. We will also require return of all keys, computers, and computer equipment, and all tools to be submitted to your supervisor before you will be given your last paycheck. If anything is lost or damaged, the cost for replacement will be deducted from your pay or recovered through the courts.

You should check your state laws if you have questions regarding collecting company materials and collecting what, if anything, the employee owes the company.

8

PAID TIME OFF (PTO)

During orientation, you need to cover PTO time with your employees as well as including it in the handbook. Legally you are not required to offer your employees PTO time. However, unless you want a discrimination lawsuit, you will need to make PTO available to everyone under the same terms. Take a look at a sample PTO schedule:

0–2 years	10 paid vacation days per year
2–4 years	12 paid vacation days per year
4–10 years	20 paid vacation days per year
10 or more years	30 paid vacation days per year

Often employers will offer a PTO schedule based on the number of hours worked in a pay period. For example, some employers will allow the employee to earn four cumulative hours of vacation per pay period.

In some states, it is illegal for the employer to take away vacation time earned if the employee does not use it. For example, if you have an employee who earns 20 paid vacation days for four years and decides to take 80 days vacation, some states approve with stipulations. To be sure you are following your state laws, check with your state's department of labor. Along with vacation rules, list the holidays your company observes. Take a look at the example below:

TLZ Enterprises is Open 360 Days a Year.

We close for Easter, Christmas, Thanksgiving, New Years Day, and the Fourth of July.

Holidays run from midnight to midnight. Therefore, if you are scheduled for a 6 p.m. to 2 a.m. shift on Christmas Day, you would report at midnight and work until 2 a.m. If you have questions, please ask your supervisor.

You will find some employers parcel the number of paid days off into sick leave, personal, and vacation time. A more complete vacation and PTO package allows PTO to accrue and be used as needed. As the employer, you should make your company policy widely known. Will you allow the PTO time to be used for sick leave or will you use a separate policy? Decide what you want to do and then enforce it uniformly with all employees:

Sick Leave

Sick days are part of your PTO package. If you are sick and have accrued PTO time, you may use the PTO for sick leave. We would appreciate a 24-hour notice if at all possible.

If you have a separate sick-leave policy enforced for all employees, you may wish to prohibit a carry-over from one year to the next or you may allow the accrual of so many days per year. However, discuss options with your team leaders and supervisors as your choice may affect production.

When discussing sick leave, if you choose to implement a separate policy from the general PTO time, you may have to stipulate the general guidelines of your policy as to whether sick leave can be used for the employee only or if it is to care for a family member as well. Think about how you want your employees to use their sick leave and then describe it in the handbook.

ACCRUED PTO

If you are going to use the modern-day PTO, you need to be sure you have checked the laws in your state. Check some options below:

> As an employee of Kinder Care, you are not allowed to accrue more than 20 hours of PTO time per calendar year. After you have reached your maximum allowable hours of PTO, you should take your paid time off so that your balance does not exceed 20 hours.

Before you decide about the accrual of PTO time, keep in mind your employees have earned the right to accrue their PTO. If you choose to make them use it, but they feel they cannot take the time away from work, you should consider paying them for their unused portion of PTO time. If you adopt this policy, the following statement should be sufficient to use in your handbook:

> Any employee who does not have the opportunity to use accrued PTO time may cash it in at the end of the year or may carry over up to 20 hours into the following year.

FAMILY AND MEDICAL LEAVE

You need to adopt and address the policy of family and medical leave with your employees. It is crucial to your success as a company because it affects the quality of employees your company will attract. Take a look at the following:

Family and Medical Leave

If you have worked for our company as a full-time employee for more than two years, we extend to you unpaid family and medical leave for the following:

- Maternity leave up to 12 weeks following delivery.

- Leave for your own serious illness—as much time as deemed necessary with a written excuse from a physician.

- Leave to care for a family member who is seriously ill—as much time as deemed necessary with a written excuse from a physician.

Additionally, in the case of the death of an immediate family member, you will be given two weeks paid time off.

Your policy for extended family and medical leave should be clearly stated and not altered because a change may result in legal problems.

You need to separate the family, medical, and bereavement leave from other types of leave if you are a company of 25 or more employees. You should be able to cover the person who has a family or medical emergency with proper staffing, and describing your policy will help to shield your company from employee suits.

PUBLIC DUTIES

If your employees are called for military or jury duty, the laws of our country mandate that you be supportive. Research laws pertaining to such leave issues and complete your policy with the law as your guide.

Voting is another duty we have as citizens but in most cases, the polls stay open to ensure citizens always have the opportunity to vote before or after work. However, if you want to allow your employees time away from work to vote, you should say so in your handbook.

9

PERFORMANCE AND BEHAVIOR ON THE JOB

Even if you employ adults, you will need to address issues of performance and behavior in the work place. You may to want to use a brief statement covering the areas that need to be addressed but you do want your employees know that you have certain standards that you expect them to follow.

PERFORMANCE ON THE JOB

If you want to ensure you have employees you can trust to perform, the best system to use is customer evaluations and reviews from your clients. You can also use a review system by one or more supervisors if you wish. However, you will need to be practical and understand that some supervisors will not get along with some employees meaning you should not put total faith in internal reviews.

In your handbook, you will want to let your employees know how and when they will be evaluated. An exception would be evaluations by mystery shoppers at unpredictable times. In such a case, your employees only need to know how they will be evaluated and nothing more. Take a look at this wording:

> At Star Burgers, we know our employees determine what our customers think of Star Burger. That is why we find it necessary to gain complete performance reviews from our customers. We use mystery shoppers to test the performance and quality of our employees, food, and service. If you have a concern about your evaluations from our mystery shoppers, please take the time to ask, and we will be happy to discuss them with you.

As the employer, you may want to hold every employee of your company accountable for his or her own performance to the extreme. Take a look at the following:

> Your job performance is crucial for the success of our company. We know if you are performing well, we perform well and when we perform well, we know we owe it to you. Poor performance at this company is unacceptable and if we have any employee who demonstrates poor performance, it will lead to discharge of employment. We remind all employees that employment is "at-will."

During training, it is important for you to convey to new employees the importance of their job performance. If you let them know what you expect, you should be able to retain more employees with higher levels of performance.

BEHAVIOR OF THE EMPLOYEE

You expect everyone to maintain good work ethics, great people skills, professional demeanor, exceptional grooming, punctuality, and attendance. However, it is necessary to post or include in your handbook your feelings about professionalism in your working environment and include all aspects of the ideal person you want working for your company. Take note of the following wording about professional behavior:

We Want Professionals Working for Frank's Shoes

At Frank's Shoes, we know sometimes employees find it difficult to get along in the work place. However, how the public sees Frank's Shoes is important to this company. How you handle yourself in the workplace is crucial to your continued employment. We ask that you avoid using profanity and try to refrain from telling off-color jokes. Other employees or our customers may find it offensive. With that in mind, we ask that you treat all people you contact at Frank's with respect. Be helpful to your co-workers and our customers. If you have a problem, do not let it brew; take care of it promptly with a supervisor or manager. We want you to have a great experience while working with us. Do your part to make that happen and we will do ours.

You may be tempted to ask your employees to behave in a professional manner both on the clock and off. Some companies have pushed the envelope a bit too far regarding what they want to know about their employees outside the work place. Laws prohibit an overbearing employer nosing into an employee's life outside the workplace. Your employees do not want a dictator, but they need an employer and there are plenty of others around if you become Little Hitler and try to enforce workplace rules outside the workplace.

CODE OF CONDUCT

Professional employees, those whose everyday judgment-calls have repercussions throughout the place of employment and directly affect the lives and livelihood of others, may be insulted by being presented a formal code of conduct. Such a code, however, is normal in some professions, such as teaching or in the military, and may need to be drawn up for those in your company who deal with the public, stating standards of integrity and responsibility to others in the workplace.

If the employee is seen as a representative of the employer wherever he happens to be, he should be mindful of his public conduct. If that means the company should have a code to be able to enforce such conduct, a brief statement to that effect may be included in the handbook. The following is one part of the code of conduct of Certified Public Accountants and may serve as an example of the wording you wish to include in your specific instance.

> Integrity is an element of character fundamental to professional recognition. It is the quality from which the public trust derives and the benchmark against which a member (read: an employee) must ultimately test all decisions.

Some codes of conduct are several inches thick, but a short statement can serve well to let employees know that they are in a professional environment and their deportment is important to the company. You may simply state that employees at all levels of the company are expected to treat each other with respect and that the success of the business depends on cooperation and teamwork among all employees. Here is another simple example of a code of conduct:

> Employees are not to conduct personal or private work while on (name of company) time.
>
> Employees are not to conduct any type of selling or soliciting while on (name of company) time.
>
> Employees shall not accept any favor or gratuity during the course of business that may affect the employee's judgment or the impartial performance of duties.
>
> Employees may engage in lawful political activities on their own time. These activities shall not interfere with job duties, or be represented as the opinion or viewpoint of the (name of company).

One of the most important reasons to have the employee handbook is to ensure that staff knows what you expect of them. Toward this end, detail desired behavior (such as dress and timeliness) as well as your policies on sexual harassment, racial and sexual discrimination, use of alcohol, drugs, and tobacco in the workplace (including pre-employment screening and post-accident testing, and disciplinary procedures for infractions). While your tone should be firm, you may stress the company's need for safety and stability at the workplace.

ETHICS

While some employers go into great detail in company policies to ensure that employees accept no gifts or meals, it is impossible to spell out every instance when ethical choices present themselves. The following is a blanket statement that puts the onus on the employee to make choices that are in the best interest of himself and your company. It is short enough to be included in your handbook.

No concise written policy can cover every ethical or legal issue that we may face. A good foundation for ethical behavior consists of individual conscience, common sense, good judgment, and compliance with governmental laws and regulation, and the basic principles within which we must all operate. Should a situation arise that is not covered in (name of company's) policy or if an employee is unsure of how to handle a situation, he or she should seek guidance from any supervisor or the legal department.

BEING ON TIME AND ATTENDANCE ISSUES

When your employees fail to show up for work, address the issue in your handbook, you may find it tough to reprimand a late employee or an employee who is a no-show altogether. Emphasize the importance of good attendance and showing up on time. Explain that numerous unexplained absences or repeated tardiness can be a basis for disciplinary action or even discharge of employment. Take a look at the following as you address punctuality and attendance in your handbook:

We are a team here at KRB and we know you are an important player on our team. That is why it is crucial for you to be on time for work and to show up for your scheduled shifts. We expect you to be ready to start to work on time.

We have all missed work at some point in our lives but most of us find a way to call our employers and if you are going to be late or if you will not be able to keep your scheduled shift, we expect a phone call. You can always reach someone at (insert phone number). If you do not call, do not come back to work. The only exception to this is a death in the immediate family or a car accident on the way to work. This may sound tough, but it's our policy. We hope you understand. In a production driven business, we need you here and we need you on time. If you cannot make it, let us know so we can get someone to fill in until you arrive.

GROOMING, DRESS, AND HYGIENE

You may need to address grooming, dress, and personal hygiene concerns during orientation. You should skim over it lightly because you are an employer of adults. Leave explicit expectations to your handbook in case there are ever any questions about appearance.

Employee Appearance

It can become heated in the plant so you will need to be dressed for comfort and for heat even in the winter months. However, tank tops are not acceptable in our workplace, and both women and men should use common sense when wearing shorts and fitted shirts. We recommend closed-toe shoes as well.

The above is an example of one policy for a laid-back dress environment in a manufacturing plant. However, you may choose to use various phrases concerning dress, grooming, and hygiene. Remember, when in doubt, keep it simple. Take a look:

We provide uniforms for our employees at Grouchy Dogs. We expect all employees to keep their uniforms clean and ironed, making for a nice appearance on the floor of the restaurant. If you have shoulder length hair or longer, it must be worn up in a ponytail or other style off the shoulders and we appreciate all employees' attention to good personal hygiene.

NO TOLERANCE

As an employer, you want to make your work place safe and comfortable for all employees. If you do not do this, you are setting yourself and your company up for failure and for ongoing legal issues. Use the handbook to pass along your policy regarding horseplay, abusive language, and fighting or bickering among employees. See below:

> We have a family atmosphere here. If you find you cannot get along with someone you are working with, please see your supervisor. We do not tolerate fighting or bickering between employees. If this happens, both parties concerned are subject to discharge.

You may want to be sure to address horseplay as well. If you have a lot of younger employees, this will need to be vocalized as well as included in your handbook. Take a look:

> We do not allow horseplay in our plant as it takes time away from production and someone else is doing your job while you take a quick break for fun. Keep the horseplay to a minimum and only outside of the plant on your own time.

Congratulations!

You have made it to the final part of this guide, Creating Your Employee Handbook!

You now have a completed employee handbook ready to be reviewed and implemented for your company. All your hard work has finally paid off.

The next step is to take everything that you have written, compile it into an attractive format, review it, get it approved, and distribute it to your employees—and most importantly, implement the policies contained in the employee handbook in a consistent and fair manner across the board for all employees. The next section of our guide will assist you with this process.

APPENDIX A

FORMS

In this section you will find sample forms that you can copy and tweak to suit your needs for your company. In the previous sections we have already discussed many of these forms, but we have provided them all to you here in one place for future reference. You can also find all the forms on the companion CD-ROM.

There should be a section in your handbook specifically for the company's current forms so that employees do not have to contact HR or manager with simple requests. For example, if an employee changes bank account information, they can simply make a copy of the direct deposit enrollment form, fill it out, and submit it to the appropriate person for updating.

Some of the forms in this section will be filled out only one time and a copy will be filed to acknowledge the employee's receipt and understanding of the policy. Having these forms in one location in the employee handbook ensures that the staff member will always have their own copy to refer to should they need to refresh their memory or clarify an issue.

This section is by no means all inclusive of the forms you may want to use for your company and staff. Add your company's forms to this section for examples and quick reference by the employee, giving employees a source for a clean form if they need to make copies for future use. Some samples of other forms that might be included here:

- Check Authorization and Approval Forms

- Sales Reports

- Employee Schedules

- Overtime Approval Forms

- Safety Equipment Check Out Forms

- Any other form that your company may use on a regularly basis

In the next pages, you will find some sample copies of forms referred to throughout the text of this guide. These forms are generic and should be tailored to the needs of your specific business.

Employee Handbook Acknowledgement

My signature below acknowledges I have received a copy of the company's employee handbook and that I understand it is my responsibility to read it.

I also acknowledge and understand that no part of this handbook constitutes a promise or contract for continued employment. My signature below acknowledges that I understand that my employment with the company is "at will" and that I or my employer can terminate or end the employment relationship at any time and for any reason allowable by law, with or without reason and with or without notice or severance compensation of any kind.

I understand that no one can alter the employment relationship through verbal contract and that the only modifications to the employment relationship must be in writing, signed by executive management and the human resources director and myself, and that in absence of any written documentation to the contrary, my employment will continue to be at will.

I understand and acknowledge that the company has the right, without prior notice, to modify, amend, or terminate policies, practices, benefit plans, and other programs within the limits and requirements imposed by law. The company will make all reasonable efforts to notify employees of any changes to policies or this handbook as soon as possible, via written communication or updates to this handbook.

_____   _____
Employee's Signature   Date

_____   _____
Employee's Name (Print)   Title

Direct Deposit Authorization Form

I hereby authorize (company name) to initiate automatic deposits to my account at the financial institution named below. I also authorize (company name) to make withdrawals from this account in the event that a credit entry is made in error.

Further, I agree not to hold (company name) responsible for any delay or loss of funds due to incorrect or incomplete information supplied by me or by my financial institution or due to an error on the part of my financial institution in depositing funds to my account.

Account Information

Financial Institution:

Routing Number:

Account Number:

Account Type: ☐ Checking   ☐ Savings

Signature

Authorized Signature

(Primary):

Date:

Authorized Signature

(Joint):

Date:

Please attach a voided check or deposit slip and return this form to the Payroll Department.

Internet Policy Acknowledgment Form

My signature on this form indicates that I have read the company's Internet policies, and I agree to abide by their terms. I understand that the company reserves the right to monitor my Internet use, and that such monitoring may occur at any time for any reason.

Printed Name

Employee's Signature   Date

The above form may be adapted to address telephone use to restrict it to business calls only.

Technology Use Policy

Section One: Purpose

To remain competitive, serve our customers well and provide our employees with the best tools to do their jobs, (name of business or owner of computer system) makes available to our workforce access to one or more forms of electronic media and services, including computers, e-mail, telephones, voice mail, fax machines, external electronic bulletin boards, wire services, online services, intranet, Internet, and the World Wide Web.

Voice Mail

Voice Mail should be used as a customer service tool. Employees who have voice mail service are expected to keep their greeting current, retrieve messages frequently, return calls promptly, and not use it as a means of avoiding answering the telephone.

Cell Phones

Company-issued cell phones should be used for essential business-related calls and never when other phones are readily available. Managers/supervisors will review monthly cell phone billings. If your cell phone is lost or stolen, you should report it immediately to your manager/supervisor.

Cell phone usage is prohibited while driving a company vehicle. You must pull off the road and park before making or receiving cellular phone calls.

Pagers

Pagers may be assigned to certain employees for company business.

Guidelines for E-mail and Internet Use

(Name of business or owner of computer system) encourages the use of these media and associated services because they can make communication more efficient and effective and because they are valuable sources of information about vendors, customers, technology, and new products and services. However, all employees and everyone connected with the organization should remember that electronic media and services provided by the company are company property and their purpose is to facilitate and support company business. All computer users have the responsibility to use these resources in a professional, ethical, and lawful manner.

To ensure that all employees are responsible, the following guidelines have been established for using e-mail and the Internet. No policy can lay down rules to cover every possible situation. Instead, it is designed to express (name of business or owner of computer system's) philosophy and set forth general principles when using electronic media and services.

Prohibited Communications

Electronic media cannot be used for knowingly transmitting, retrieving, or storing any communication that is:

Discriminatory or harassing; Derogatory to any individual or group;

Obscene, sexually explicit, or pornographic; Defamatory or threatening;

In violation of any license governing the use of software; or Engaged in for any purpose that is illegal or contrary to _____ (name of business or owner of computer system's) policy or business interests.

Personal Use

The computers, electronic media, and services provided by (name of business or owner of computer system) are primarily for business use to assist employees in the performance of their jobs. Limited, occasional, or incidental use of electronic media (sending or receiving) for personal, non-business purposes is understandable and acceptable, and all such use should be done in a manner that does not negatively affect the systems' use for business purposes. However, employees are expected to demonstrate a sense of responsibility and not abuse this privilege.

Access to Employee Communications

Generally, electronic information created or communicated by an employee using e-mail, word processing, utility programs, spreadsheets, voice e-mail, telephones, Internet and bulletin board system access, and similar electronic media is not reviewed by the company. However, the following conditions should be noted:

(Name of business or owner of computer system) does routinely gather logs for most electronic activities or monitor employee communications directly, e.g., telephone numbers dialed, sites accessed, call length, and time calls are made, for the following purposes:

Cost analysis;

Resource allocation;

Optimum technical management of information resources; and

Detecting patterns of use that indicate employees are violating company policies or engaging in illegal activity.

(Name of business or owner of computer system) reserves the right, at its discretion, to review any employee's electronic files and messages to the extent necessary to ensure electronic media and services are being used in compliance with the law, this policy, and other company policies. Employees should not assume electronic communications are completely private. Accordingly, if they have sensitive information to transmit, they should use other means.

Software

To prevent viruses from being transmitted through the company's computer system, downloading of any unauthorized software is strictly prohibited. Only software registered through (name of business or owner of computer system) may be downloaded. Employees should contact the system administrator if they have any questions.

Security/Appropriate Use

Employees must respect the confidentiality of other individuals' electronic communications. Except when explicit authorization has been granted by company management, employees are prohibited from engaging in, or attempting to engage in:

Monitoring or intercepting the files or electronic communications of other employees or third parties;

Hacking or obtaining access to systems or accounts they are not authorized to use;

Using other people's log-ins or passwords; and

Breaching, testing, or monitoring computer or network security measures.

No e-mail or other electronic communication can be sent that attempts to hide the identity of the sender or represent the sender as someone else.

Electronic media and services should not be used in a manner likely to cause network congestion or significantly hamper the ability of other people to access and use the system.

Anyone obtaining electronic assess to other companies' or individuals' materials must respect all copyrights and cannot copy, retrieve, modify, or forward copyrighted materials except as permitted by the copyright owner.

Encryption

Employees can use encryption software supplied to them by the systems administrator for purposes of safeguarding sensitive or confidential business information. Employees who use encryption on files stored on a company computer must provide their supervisor with a sealed hard copy record (to be retained in a secure location) of all of the passwords and encryption keys necessary to access the files.

Participation in Online Forums

Any messages or information sent on company-provided facilities to one or more individuals via an electronic network—for example, Internet mailing lists, bulletin boards, and online services—are statements identifiable and attributable to (name of business or owner of computer system).

(Name of business or owner of computer system) recognizes that participation in some forums might be important to the performance of an employee's job. For instance, an employee might find the answer to a technical problem by consulting members of a news group devoted to the technical area.

Violations

Any employee who abuses the privilege of their access to e-mail or the Internet in violation of this policy will be subject to corrective action, including possible discharge of employment, legal action, and criminal liability.

Employee Agreement on Use of E-mail and the Internet

I have read, understand, and agree to comply with the foregoing policies, rules, and conditions governing the use of the company's computer and telecommunications equipment and services. I understand that I have no expectation of privacy when I use any of the telecommunication equipment or services. I am aware that violations of this guideline on appropriate use of the e-mail and Internet systems may subject me to disciplinary action, including discharge from employment, legal action, and criminal liability. I further understand that my use of the e-mail and Internet may reflect on the image of (name of business or owner of computer system) to our customers, competitors, and suppliers and that I have responsibility to maintain a positive representation of the company. Furthermore, I understand that this policy can be amended at any time.

Employee Signature: Date:

Employee Computer Account Number:

Sample Time Sheet/Time Card

Hourly Employee Time Sheet

(name of company)

(Company Address)

(Company Address)

(Company Telephone Number)

(Company Fax Number)

Employee Name:

Employee Title:

Employee Number:

Department:

Supervisor:

Day		Regular Hours	Over-time Hours	Sick	Vacation	Total
Monday	11/1					
Tuesday	11/2					
Wednesday	11/3					
Thursday	11/4					
Friday	11/5					
Saturday	11/6					
Sunday	11/7					
Monday	11/8					
Tuesday	11/9					
Wednesday	11/10					
Thursday	11/11					
Friday	11/12					
Saturday	11/13					
Sunday	11/14					
	Total hours					
	Rate (Regular/ Overtime)					
	Total pay					

All employee time cards are to be turned in no later than (time) on (day). Employee time cards can be faxed into the (company name) or mailed to the address listed above. If you have any questions on how to fill out your time card, please contact your supervisor or the Human Resource Department.

APPENDIX B

PUTTING TOGETHER AND DISTRIBUTING YOUR EMPLOYEE HANDBOOK

The handbook is finished. Now what?

Compile your material into one finished product. Do one last proofread and edit and print the text of the handbook. At this point it is a good idea to have another set of eyes review the document for any errors. Remember, an employee handbook is often the first introduction to the company that an employee receives and you do not want to introduce your company in a sloppy and inefficient manner.

After the handbook has been edited and proofread, you can now print a "proof" version to submit for approval. Your company's owner, board of directors, or operations manager, or HR director (or perhaps all) will need to sign off on the handbook before it is implemented,

After everyone has reviewed it, make any necessary changes, and now you are ready for your final steps in this process.

LEGALITIES

Have your finished handbook reviewed by an attorney who is familiar with labor relations. Only an attorney or legal advisor can be certain that your policies and language conform to the laws in your company's location(s). Time and money spent now to ensure the handbook is 100 percent legal for your company could save thousands of dollars in legal and court costs later.

PRESENTATION

For a more attractive and appealing employee handbook, you can choose to add a title page and a cover page for each section. If you include a mini-table of contents keep in mind that if you update your handbook at any time, the cover pages for each section will need to be updated as well.

Color copying, professional printing, pictures, and graphics are an inviting, attractive addition to your handbook, but they can be expensive. If cost is a factor, but you still want to spice up the look of the handbook, you may consider using black and white graphics, text boxes, and relevant quotations to fill up some of the white space in your handbook. (People like interesting quotes, quips, or amusing anecdotes. Adding such filler might even encourage the employees to flip through the book just to read these tidbits, and by default, they may actually read more of the handbook.)

FORMATTING

The next step is to format the book into, well, a book, and then after that, distribute it to your employees.

While you could just print all of the pages and hand them to the new employee, you need to keep in mind that your employee handbook is the first introduction to the company that a new employee sees. It should accurately reflect the culture and attitude of the company.

It does not have to cost a lot of money to create an employee handbook. As you can see, the final product is not actually a great number of pages, and you can use your own office equipment to make copies, or if you have a large staff, you can get a small print shop to make all of the copies for your staff with several extras for new hires.

You may want to include a set of dividers with tabs if you are copying the handbook in-house. Office supply stores have them along with other items that provide color and interest to an otherwise drab looking booklet.

The following two options will create an appealing look for the handbook, but they are not encouraged because of the cost and expense of updating it. You may have a printer or print shop punch and bind your handbook. Some companies may already have the equipment to bind the handbook in-house. If budget is not an issue, your company may even consider having the book soft-cover bound at a print shop.

After the first section has been placed in your handbook, you then can add the divider for section two and then all the policies covered in that section behind it, and then continue doing this for all sections of the handbook until each one is placed in the binder.

Each section of the handbook has been assigned a number. That number corresponds to the chapter of the handbook, or in this case, the tab on the divider. For example, in Section One you have five different policies all pertaining to the introduction and welcome of the company. You would place the divider marked "1" in front of all the pages of text for section one.

Each policy (i.e. 1.1, 1.2, 1.3, etc.) may have its own page. Each new sub-section should begin on its own page.

After you have finished placing all the pages behind each of the dividers and have put all that into the binder you have selected, you now have a completed employee handbook.

HOW TO DISTRIBUTE YOUR HANDBOOK

Now that your handbook has been written, reviewed, and approved, what do you do with it? A handbook can only work if you get it out to your employees in a timely manner. For new employees, this is easy. You will simply give the employee handbook to the employee on or before their first day on the job. After you give the handbook to the new hire, be sure to get them to sign the Employee Handbook Acknowledgement Form and place a copy of this in their employee file immediately.

If you are implementing a handbook for the first time, or have completely revamped your existing employee handbook and need to distribute it to all of your employees, you have a bit more of a challenge. For small businesses where all employees are in one location, this may be an easy task. You simply pass the handbook out to each employee and have them sign the acknowledgement form right then.

However, if your company is a bit larger, handing them out might be a daunting task. Because an employee handbook is the company's way of communicating new policies to employees, some of these items having legal repercussions, it is imperative that you ensure every employee has been issued a handbook and that you have a signed acknowledgment form on file for each person.

There is another legal issue that might also be considered here as well. If you have contractors working for your company, either independently or through a staffing or placement agency, your company should not present an employee handbook directly to that contractor. While it is important that the contractor have some of the information in that handbook, not all of it pertains to a contract employee.

If the employee is through a staffing or placement agency, you should have the manager or human resources professional responsible for dealing with that agency contact the agency and present the handbook to the agency, not the contractor. The agency is responsible for the employee, not your company. When the agents have a copy of the handbook, they can review the information themselves and discuss it with the employee without jeopardizing their contractor status. Providing a copy directly to the contractor may be construed as providing that contractor with the status of "employee" and if that contractor were to take your company to court, your company could well be responsible for providing benefits and back compensation to the contractor equal to that of a employee.

It is important to know which employees on your staff have been hired under a contract. Hiring contracts differ in the terms and conditions of employment than the generic policies in this employee handbook. An executive level manager may have been hired with an agreement that he cannot be discharged except for cause for a set period of time, or perhaps he was offered two additional weeks of vacation per year over that of a non-contracted employee.

It is important to provide a letter or some other terminology, perhaps even included in the employee handbook itself, that if the employee has a hiring contract signed by the appropriate personnel, the contract supersedes information in the handbook particularly in benefits information. It is also important that the contracted employee understand that all sections of the employee handbook not specifically addressed in their hiring contract do, in fact, pertain to them, too.

The first step is to acquire a list of all employees in the company from human resources and categorize it into sections: contractors, contracted employees, nonexempt, and exempt.

One option is to provide the same handbook to all employees with information for exempt and nonexempt, hourly, and salaried employees and let the employees determine which policies pertain to them, or you may wish to have two handbooks, particularly if benefits are drastically different. The choice depends on how much the policies, especially in terms of benefits, differ between the two classes of employees and whether you want your employees to know how much they differ.

For example, hourly or nonexempt employees may only accrue one week vacation time per year while salaried or exempt employees may accrue two weeks per year. Perhaps hourly employees must keep time sheets and are docked pay for each hour they miss, while salaried employees are only docked pay if they are gone more than four hours during the work day. Maybe your hourly employees and salaried employees are provided different retirement or insurance plans.

Now that you have your employee list, you need to find a systematic way to distribute the handbook to everyone. If your company has mailboxes for each staff member, this is a quick and easy way to distribute the book, but you still face the issue of having to collect the acknowledgment forms back from each employee. Another way would be to e-mail each employee and request that they come by and pick up a copy of the handbook by a certain date, and when they do, be sure to get their signature at that time.

Using your employee list, you can check off all employees who picked up their handbooks and signed the acknowledgement forms. This way, you can follow up with any stragglers who have not yet come to pick up their handbooks. Simply continue this cycle until you have received an acknowledgement form from each employee.

For larger companies with a large employee base, you may want to contact department or division managers and make them responsible for distributing the book to the employees and returning the acknowledgement forms. Another suggestion, if you are not interested in distributing the handbook immediately, is to provide the handbook to each employee at performance review time.

ALTERNATIVE DISTRIBUTION IDEAS

With the Internet and technology becoming so popular, most companies have a Web site presence. It is possible to have your employee handbook available to view or download online via a company intranet or via an employees' section of the Web site. Depending on the complexity of your Web site, you may even be able to send out an electronic notice, or e-mail, to every employee in the system and have them "electronically or digitally sign" the acknowledgement form.

Using the Internet to have an online employee handbook is a creative and effective way to manage an employee handbook, but we still recommend providing a written hard copy to all employees as well, because not all employees may be given computer authorization or access.

The Internet site can be used for quick reference, be searchable, and give the ability to print forms or other information at a moment's notice. It also helps to ensure that handbook updates are not missed. You may provide a hard copy update to your employee, but perhaps it gets lost in the shuffle.

Using the company bulletin board, if you have one, is also a good place to post notices of update and changes to policies in the employee handbook, along with instructions on how to receive a copy of the changes should the employee have missed it.

One last idea for distributing your handbook that might be cost effective is to provide the handbook in hard copy to those employees who do not have access to a computer or who request a hard copy, but providing a CD-ROM in PDF format to those employees who have computer access. PDF format allows the user to view and print the files without being able to make any changes to the original documents or text in the file.

HOW TO UPDATE YOUR HANDBOOK

Now that you have your employee handbook completed and you have distributed it to your employees, it is important that someone be assigned to ensure that your handbook is up-to-date and current.

Check regularly to ensure compliance with any legal changes that may affect the employee-employer relationship in any way. Anti-discrimination laws often change, including different protected statuses, or perhaps a new government reporting requirement is added. Any number of other rules, regulations, and laws that may affect your company may occur with no publicity or notice to your company. In Appendix C we provide resources your company can use to keep up-to-date on any developments that may change your handbook policies.

Company-wide changes in policy may arise from implementation difficulties of some policies. Perhaps the company has grown and it is not able to provide health insurance as a group benefit to its employees where no health insurance was available before. There are any number of reasons why a policy might need to be added or changed in your company's employee handbook, but the important part is keeping up with those changes and ensuring that the handbook is the most current it can be.

One way to communicate with employees is through memo updates. Memos may not necessarily be specific policy updates, but any memo can affect the employee-employer relationship without actually requiring a policy change. Memos can also be used to update employees in the interim between normal update periods. For example, if the policy needs to be changed, the company can choose to change policies once per year. In the meantime, a memo can be issued to the employee about a policy update or change.

If you decide to do updates in this manner, you may want to include a clause in your employee handbook about memo updates and include a tab at the back of the book for the employee to file the updates in the order they are received. At the end of the year, you can update the entire handbook by printing out only the policy changes or additions and distributing them to employees to add to their copy of employee handbook.

For this reason, it is not recommended that the employee handbook have page numbers. There are few pages in each section, so that tab dividers are really all that is necessary. If you feel you must number the pages, consider numbering them inside each section. For example, behind tab divider number one, you would have section one of the handbook, beginning with page one and proceeding to page five. Then behind tab divider number two, you have section number two of the handbook, beginning with page one and going to page two. This way, if you do have to update or add or change a policy, you will only need to reprint and update one section at a time.

When it is time to update a policy and make an addition, deletion, or a change to the handbook, you simply open the original handbook file and make changes. Next, print out the changed version, only printing the sections affected by the change. Third, prepare a memo to the staff to attach to the amended sections of the employee handbook with instructions to the employee on how to update their own handbook.

If you are reprinting all of Section Three of the employee handbook, your instructions would ask the employee to remove Section Three, destroy the original, and replace that section with the new copy attached. If you are only updating a portion of the section, spell out exactly which policy is being changed and ask employees to update their handbook with the new pages.

If you require some kind of confirmation that the employee has received the update, you can follow the same verification procedure you used when you originally requested the acknowledgment forms from the employee.

On the next page you will find a sample memo for instructing your employees to update their employee handbook. Note one important factor on this memo: it should be initialed and approved by the appropriate staff members. Remember, you told the employees in your handbook that no one could modify and alter the policies in this handbook except for_____ _____ and _____, so to be true to that policy. You need to be sure that the person or people listed in the approval sections of the handbook have signed the memo for the update.

That brings us to another reason that an employee handbook might need to be updated. If there is now a different person who is responsible for approving changes or if there is a change in positions or the chain of command, this information should be added to the handbook as well.

It sounds like extra work, but it is really not all that complicated after the handbook has been implemented. Reviewing the handbook once a month, just to ensure the information is current will not take too much out of the day, and it can save a world of future problems if the information in the handbook were to become outdated, or worse, illegal.

Again, an employee handbook is not a replacement for effectively communicating in person with the employees of the company, but it is an important tool in the communication process.

Immediate Update to Employee Handbook

Included with this memo is a critical update to the employee handbook. There has been a change in the law that is pertinent to Section Three of your employee handbook. The federal government has added the protected status of "sexual orientation" to the anti-discrimination laws. Our policy has been updated to include this status in our terminology in this section so that we are in compliance with law. Please remove the entire Section Three from your handbook and replace it with the pages included with this memo, in its entirety.

Thank you.

APPENDIX C

WHERE TO LOOK FOR STATE SPECIFIC LAWS

http://www.eeoc.gov/

http://www.bls.gov/

Administrative Review Board (ARB)

Benefits Review Board (BRB)

Bureau of International Labor Affairs (ILAB)

Bureau of Labor Statistics (BLS)

Center for Faith-Based & Community Initiatives

Employees' Compensation Appeals Board (ECAB)

Employment Standards Administration (ESA)

Office of Federal Contract Compliance Programs (OFCCP)

The Office of Labor-Management Standards (OLMS)

Office of Worker's Compensation Programs (OWCP)

Wage and Hour Division (WHD)

Mine Safety & Health Administration (MSHA)

Employment & Training Administration (ETA)

Occupational Safety & Health Administration (OSHA)

Employee Benefits Security Administration (EBSA)

Veterans' Employment & Training Service (VETS)

Women's Bureau (WB)

Other Organizational Units Within the Department

Presidential Task Force on Employment of Adults With Disabilities (PTFEAD)

Office of Administrative Law Judges (OALJ)

Office of Congressional & Intergovernmental Affairs (OCIA)

Office of the Assistant Secretary for Administration and Management (OASAM)

Office of the Assistant Secretary for Policy (OASP)

Office of the Chief Financial Officer (OCFO)

Office of the Chief Information Officer (OCIO)

Office of Disability Employment Policy (ODEP)

Office of Inspector General (OIG)

Office of Small business Programs (OSBP)

Office of the Solicitor (SOL)

Office of the Secretary (OSEC)

Office of the 21st Century Workforce (21CW)

Related Legislation

1931 – Davis-Bacon Act

1938 – Fair Labor Standards Act

1946 – Employment Act PL 79-304

1949 – Fair Labor Standards Amendment PL 81–393

1953 – Small Business Act PL 83–163

1954 – Internal Revenue Code PL 83–591

1955 – Fair Labor Standards Amendment PL 84–381

1958 – Small Business Administration extension PL 85–536

1961 – Fair Labor Standards Amendment PL 87–30

1961 – Area Redevelopment Act PL 87–27

1962 – Manpower Development and Training Act PL 87–415

1962 – Public Welfare Amendments PL 87–543

1963 – Amendments to National Defense Education Act PL 88–210

1964 – Economic Opportunity Act PL 88–452

1965 – Vocational Rehabilitation Act amended PL 89–333

1966 – Fair Labor Standards Amendment PL 89–601

1967 – Executive Order 11246

1973 – Comprehensive Employment and Training Act PL 93–203

1973 – Section 503 of the Rehabilitation Act PL 93–112

1974 – Fair Labor Standards Amendment PL 93–259

1974 – Vietnam Era Veterans' Readjustment Assistance Act PL 92–540

1975 – Revenue Adjustment Act (Earned Income Tax Credit) PL 94–12, 164

1976 – Overhaul of Vocational Education programs PL 94–482

1976 – Social Security Act Amendments (Aid to Day Care Centers) PL 94–401

1977 – Fair Labor Standards Amendment PL 95–151

1978 – Full Employment and Balanced Growth Act PL 95–523

1981 – Budget Reconciliation Act PL 97–35

1982 – Job Training Partnership Act PL 97–300

1986 – Migrant and Seasonal Agricultural Worker Protection Act PL 99–603

1988 – Family Support Act PL 100–485

1989 – Fair Labor Standards Amendment PL 101–157

1990 – Omnibus Budget Reconciliation Act PL 101–508

1993 – Omnibus Budget Reconciliation and Bankruptcy Act PL 103–66

1996 – Small Business Job Protection Act PL 104–188

1996 – Personal Responsibility and Work Opportunity Reconciliation Act PL 104–Veterans Employment Opportunities Act PL 105–339

http://en.wikipedia.org/wiki/United_States_Department_of_Labor

APPENDIX D

HANDBOOK SAMPLES

Following, you will find two different samples. The first is a complete Employee Handbook for a fictional business named Lane's Garden. Comments and suggestions have been added in italic after various sections to help you identify additional ways to customize your handbook.

The first sample also depicts tabbed dividers used to break up the sections for quick and easy access. These dividers can be professionally done by the printer or if you are copying and printing your handbook yourself, your copier may have a feature for numbering or naming tabbed dividers. You can also buy numbered dividers in various colors and sizes at most office supply stores.

The second is a sample of a handbook that could easily be adapted by a mom and pop business. Both of these samples are formatted for easy reference so employees will be able to locate the information they need when they need it.

EMPLOYEE HANDBOOK

829 South August Street

Bloomingburg, WI 54766

Use your company name, logo, or a picture relevant to your company to make the cover attractive.

WELCOME

We are pleased to welcome you and hope you will find your position and duties here pleasant, challenging, and rewarding. Our employees are the most talented and creative individuals in the industry, and we are proud to welcome you to our team. Please take the time to review this section of your employee handbook where we will provide you with some company background information, history, our vision and mission, and introduce you to our culture and environment so you can feel comfortable and understand the nature of your new workplace.

We are excited to have you aboard and look forward to a successful and productive working relationship. Congratulations on your new career with Lane's Garden.

MISSION STATEMENT

Lane's Garden strives to be an innovative leader in floral arrangement and gifts serving the greater Bloomingburg area.

We are committed to beautifying the gardens and homes of our customers throughout the seasons by providing a wide selection of high quality products and services, along with friendly, knowledgeable staff.

It is the goal of this company to make every visit to Lane's Garden a pleasant experience for the whole family while providing a fun and rewarding place to shop, work and do business.

INTRODUCTION

COMPANY HISTORY

Lane's Garden, was founded in 2000 by twin sisters Mary and Julie Vandercless. Mary spent 30 years as an upper level manager and handles the financial and business side of Lane's Garden. Julie, with a degree in horticulture and art, handles the more creative details. Lane's Garden currently has a staff of 28 full and part-time employees.

Tips for the Information Section

In this section, you may want to expand and include more information on:

- *Your company's history.*

- *A description of your company culture and corporate environment.*

- *Definitions and explanations of the company's values and standards for customer services, client relations, employee relationships, product or services, quality and standards. Be clear and concise in stating the company's values because you expect an employee to live up to them, but at the same time, make this a positive section to motivate and educate the employee on the company's has high values and standards.*

- *Company, department, or employee goals to strive toward to achieve the values previously listed. For example, if the company values customer service, what is the goal for the employee to achieve that quality customer services?*

- *Provide information about the company's service or product and the company's place in the community.*

USING THIS HANDBOOK

INTRODUCTION

At Lane's Garden, we believe our employees feel more comfortable and valued when they clearly understand the expectations for them, as the employee, and for us, as the employer. For this reason, we are providing you this employee handbook to introduce you to the company and give you information and policies to guide you through your employment experience. The company's vision and mission should be followed in every action you take at our company. This handbook will help you achieve the goals the company expects of all its employees.

Each section of this handbook spells out certain rules, regulations, laws, and policies pertaining to the employee–employer relationship. Each section deals with a different topic and clearly spells out for you all of your benefits and responsibilities while you maintain your status as a valuable team member with Lane's Garden.

However, since we cannot possibly include every scenario or foresee all eventualities, this employee handbook is a summary of the most common employment related issues and laws. Should you not be able to find the answer to a specific question you may have, we encourage you to discuss this issue with your immediate supervisor or contact Mary Vandercless.

The information in this employee handbook and its updates supersedes all verbal information relayed to the employee. If the employee has been given verbal instructions that conflict with this employee handbook, the employee handbook is the final authority on the company policy, and the employee should follow all policies in the employee handbook at all times.

PHONE LIST

Here is the contact information for the management staff. Addresses, phone numbers and e-mail are for employee use only and should not be given out without permission. Mary Vandercless has a complete contact list for all staff, if the employee you are seeking is not listed below.

Lane's Garden
829 South August Street
Bloomingsburg, WI 54766
PH 608-788-LANE (5263) · FAX 608-788-5262
Web: www.lanesgarden.com · E-mail: info@ lanesgarden.com

Mary Vandercless
109 East May Street
Bloomingsburg, WI 54766
PH 608-788-5263 ext. 101 · Home PH: 608-788-1287
Mobile: 608-788-1288 · E-mail: mary@ lanesgarden.com

Julie Vandercless
3500 S Greg Blvd.
Bloomingsburg, WI 54766
PH 608-788-5263 ext. 102 · Home PH: 608-782-9121
Mobile: 608-788-1457 · E-mail: julie@ lanesgarden.com

You will note that this begins a new section and the binder tab has moved. If you choose to include a phone list, you should include all of your company department heads and pertinent phone numbers within the company. An employee's home telephone number should never be given out to anyone outside the workplace.

EMPLOYEE BULLETIN BOARD

Located in the employee break room you will find important information about your employment, your legal rights and responsibilities within the company, as well as all federal, state, and local employment-related posting information such as wage and labor laws. It is the company's responsibility to keep these postings accurate and up-to-date, and it is the employee's responsibility to read and understand the information relayed in these postings.

In addition to employee–employer related postings, Lane's Garden allows employees to post personal and business information on the company bulletin boards, provided the information is free from profanity or derogatory- or discriminatory language. Such postings may include meeting dates and times, garage sales, personal property for sale, and other non-competitive services/products. Please keep the bulletin board current. Any posting left longer than two weeks will be removed.

Here are some optional policies on bulletin board use you may choose to adopt instead of the example above:

- *In addition to employee/employment related postings, our company allows employees to post personal and business information on the company bulletin boards, provided the information is free from profanity or derogatory or discriminatory language. All postings to the company bulletin board must be approved by (insert name of person) and will be posted for two weeks from date of approval. Any postings placed on the board without approval will be immediately removed.*

- *This bulletin board is a useful tool to provide information and updates from management to employees. Therefore, we do not allow employees to post information on this board. Any unofficial postings will be removed. Thank you for your compliance.*

EMPLOYMENT IS "AT WILL"

EMPLOYMENT TERMS

We are pleased to welcome you to our company and hope that your employment here will be a rewarding and positive experience.

Lane's Garden is committed to your success in our workplace and we want to help you continue to grow and be satisfied with your working environment; however, we cannot make any promises or guarantees for continued employment with out company.

Lane's Garden is an "at will" employer and, therefore, your employment here is "at will" meaning that you are able to resign from your position at any time, and for any reason or no reason, without any further requirements or recrimination, just as the company is also free to terminate employment at any time and for any reason or no reason, without any notices—with or without cause.

EMPLOYMENT TERMS

LANE'S GARDEN

FLORAL & GIFTS

No part of this employee handbook constitutes, in any way, a contract or promise or guarantee of continued employment.

It is not possible for any employee to authorize a change in the employment "at will" status or to contract with any employee for terms of employment in violation of this "at will" policy without specific written consent and approval of the hiring contract by Mary Vandercless.

If you do offer employment contracts to some employees, you may want to address that in this section. Here is an example:

(Insert name of company) does offer hiring packages and hiring contracts to certain senior level executive exempt management positions. For those hiring contracts, the terms and conditions of employment are defined in your contract. In the absence of this hiring contract, employment is considered "at will," and the terms of this handbook and this policy apply.

COMMITMENT TO EQUAL EMPLOYMENT OPPORTUNITY

EQUAL EMPLOYMENT OPPORTUNITY

Lane's Garden believes all applicants and employees are entitled to equal employment opportunity. We follow all applicable local, state, and federal laws prohibiting discrimination in hiring and employment. Our company does not discriminate against applicants or employees in violation of any of these laws.

Here is a sample alternative for Equal Employment Opportunity:

Our company does not discriminate against applicants or employees on the basis of (insert all characteristics that you want to include here) or any other characteristic or status protected by local, state, or federal laws.

EMPLOYEE RECRUITMENT

Lane's Garden can only be as good as the employees selected to represent us; therefore, we search all possible avenues to recruit talented and skilled employees to fill our open positions. To achieve this diverse applicant pool we use the following methods to attract exceptional applicants including newspaper advertisements, Web site listings, job boards, professional recruiting companies.

EMPLOYEE REFERRALS

Lane's Garden also encourages employees to recruit and refer applicants from the community for open positions within the company. If an employee refers an applicant who is hired and completes at least 90 days of employment with our company, we will provide a referral bonus of $100 to the employee who referred them to us. In order to qualify for the referral program, you must fill out the Employee Referral Form and turn it in to Mary Vandercless PRIOR to the applicant beginning employment. The form must be signed by the current employee, the perspective employee and Mary Vandercless.

EMPLOYEE RECRUITMENT

EMPLOYEE PROMOTION

While Lane's Garden does look outside the company for applicants for open positions, we also recognize talents and experience of current employees who may wish to be promoted. From time to time, we may post positions internally or both externally and internally.

We will post all internal job postings on the company bulletin board located in the breakroom. If you are interested in applying for an open position, the company encourages you to apply by contacting Mary Vandercless for our internal application procedure.

EMPLOYEE RECRUITMENT

You may want to list your step by step internal procedures an employee should follow to apply for an open job posting in this section.

EMPLOYING RELATIVES—NEPOTISM

As a general rule, there are no specific company policies excluding hiring relatives for most open job postings because the applicant is related to a current employee. We encourage all applicants who are qualified for a position, regardless of their relation to a current employee, to apply for the position.

However, we do recognize that in certain situations, depending on the applicant's position and their relative's position in the company, it may be inappropriate to hire a family member because of the potential of negatively affecting the morale of other employees or creating certain conflicts of interest among the staff and relatives involved, particularly in the case where one relative would be supervising another.

Because of this possibility, we will not hire relatives of current employees for positions in which one family member would supervise another family member.

For the purposes of this policy, the term "relative" will include spouses, wives, live-in or domestic partners, parents, children, siblings, in-laws, aunts, uncles, and cousins to include relations by blood/family, marriage, or step relations.

EMPLOYMENT OF RELATIVES

If you do not hire relatives, your policy could state:

- *Our employees are valued members of our team, and therefore, we also value our employees' families as an extension of the employee; however, we have a policy against hiring family members of current employees for jobs within our company.*

ORIENTATION

NEW EMPLOYEE ORIENTATION

On your first day of employment, you will be scheduled for new employee orientation meeting. You will receive important information about our company's policies and procedures. You will also be asked to complete paperwork and forms relating to your employment, such as tax withholding forms, emergency contact forms, and benefits paperwork.

Please feel free to ask any questions you might have about the company during the orientation meeting. If additional questions come up after the meeting, you can ask your supervisor or Mary or Julie Vandercless.

ORIENTATION PERIOD

The first 90 days of your employment are an orientation period. During this time, your supervisor will work with you to help you learn how to do your job successfully and what the company expects of you. This period also provides you and the company an opportunity to decide whether you are suited for the position for which you were hired.

When your employment begins, you will meet with Mary Vandercless, who will explain our benefits and payroll procedures and assist you in completing your employment paperwork. (For our company's benefits policies, see Benefits section of this handbook.)

ORIENTATION

You will also meet with your supervisor to go over your job goals and performance requirements. During the orientation period, your supervisor will give you feedback on your performance and will be available to answer any questions you might have.

Employees are not eligible for the following benefits until they complete the orientation period:

- Medical/Life Insurance
- Retirement Plan
- Paid Holidays
- Paid Vacation
- Sick Leave

Although we hope that you will be successful here, the company may terminate your employment at any time, either during the orientation period or afterwards, with or without cause and with or without notice. You are also free to resign at any time and for any reason, either during the orientation period or afterwards, with or without notice. Successful completion of your orientation period does not guarantee you a job for any period of time or in any way change the "at-will" employment relationship.

Your orientation period may be extended if the company decides that such an extension is appropriate.

PROOF OF WORK ELIGIBILITY *(vertical side tab)*

PROOF OF WORK ELIGIBILITY

Within three business days of your first day of work, you must complete Federal Form I-9 and show us documentation proving your identity and your eligibility to work in the United States. The federal government requires us to do this.

If you have worked for this company previously, you need only provide this information if it has been more than three years since you last completed an I-9 Form for us or if your current I-9 Form is no longer valid.

Here are some optional policies on Alternative Proof of Work Eligibility

- *(Insert name of person) will give you an I–9 Form and tell you what documentation you must present to us.*

- *At your _____(insert title of meeting—for example, "new hire interview" or "orientation") you should have received a blank I-9 Form and instructions on completing it. If you did not, contact (insert name of person) immediately.*

CHILD SUPPORT REPORTING REQUIREMENTS

At Lane's Garden we follow all state of Wisconsin child support reporting requirements. This includes but is not limited to:

- Withholding begins one week after receipt of order.
- Payment is sent within 5 days of payday.
- If needed a termination notice will be sent within 10 days of termination.
- Administrative fee is $3 per payment.
- Withholding limits are according to the Federal Rules under CCPA.

These guidelines have been established according to the Department of Workforce Development, Division of Economic Support, Bureau of Child Support, 1 W. Wilson St., Rm. 382, P.O. Box 7935, Madison, WI 53707-7935

CHILD SUPPORT

PLEASE NOTE: The text of this policy depends on the specifics of your company and state law, we cannot provide you with a standard policy to use. Please see the main discussion for assistance in drafting this policy language yourself. The above is only meant to be an example.

EMPLOYEE CLASSIFICATIONS

TEMPORARY EMPLOYEES

Periodically it becomes necessary for us to hire individuals to perform a job or to work on a project that has a limited duration. Typically this happens in the event of a special project, special time of year, abnormal workload, or emergency.

These individuals are temporary employees. They are not eligible to participate in any of our company benefit programs, nor can they earn or accrue any leave, such as vacation leave or sick leave.

Of course, we will provide any benefits mandated by law to temporary employees.

Temporary employees cannot change from temporary status to any other employment status by such informal means as remaining in our employ for a long period of time or through oral promises made to them by coworkers, members of management, or supervisors. The only way a temporary employee's status can change is through a written notification signed by Mary Vandercless.

Like all employees who work for this company, temporary employees work on an "at-will" basis, meaning that both they and the company are free to terminate their employment at any time for any legal reason—even if the employee has not completed the project.

EMPLOYEE CLASSIFICATIONS

PART-TIME AND FULL-TIME EMPLOYEES

Depending on the number of hours per week you are regularly scheduled to work, you are either a part-time or a full-time employee. It is necessary that you understand which of these classifications applies to you, because it determines whether you are entitled to benefits and leave.

PART-TIME EMPLOYEES

Employees who are regularly scheduled to work fewer than 40 hours per week are part-time employees.

FULL-TIME EMPLOYEES

Employees who are regularly scheduled to work at least 40 hours per week are full-time employees.

EXEMPT AND NONEXEMPT EMPLOYEES

Your entitlement to earn overtime pay depends on whether you are classified as an exempt or a nonexempt employee.

Exempt employees are those who do not earn overtime because they are exempt from the overtime provisions of the federal Fair Labor Standards Act and applicable state laws.

Nonexempt employees are those who meet the criteria for being covered by the overtime provisions of the federal Fair Labor Standards Act and applicable state laws. If you are uncertain about which category you fall into, speak to Mary Vandercless.

HOURS OF OPERATION

Lane's Garden is open the following hours:

Monday through Friday 8 a.m. - 9 p.m.
Saturdays 9 a.m. - 6 p.m. • Sunday 12 p.m. - 5 p.m.

Hours may be subject to change during the summer and holiday season.

We typically operate in 2 shifts:

Monday through Friday from 7:30 a.m. to 4:30 p.m., from 4:30 p.m. to 9:30 p.m.

Shifts are scheduled by supervisors for weekends on a rotating basis. Your supervisor will let you know your shift assignment. If you wish to change shifts permanently, talk to your supervisor. Although the company will consider all requests to change shifts, we cannot guarantee that any particular request will be granted. You may exchange shifts with another employee (switch shifts on a one-time basis) only with the prior approval of your supervisor.

HOURS

Here are some optional policies on hours:

- *Your supervisor will provide your work schedule, including what time you will be expected to start and finish work each day.*

- *All employees are expected to be here, ready to start work when we open. Unless you make other arrangements with your supervisor, you are expected to work until closing time.*

FLEXIBLE SCHEDULING

At Lane's Garden we understand that many employees have to balance the demands of their job with the needs of their families and other outside commitments. Therefore, we offer our employees the opportunity to work a flexible schedule. If you would like to change your work schedule—for example, to come in and leave a couple of hours earlier or to work more hours on some days and fewer on others—talk to your supervisor. We will try to accommodate your request to the extent practical.

Because some jobs are unsuitable for flexible scheduling, and because we must ensure that our staffing needs are met, we cannot guarantee that the company will grant your request.

MEALS AND REST BREAKS

Employees are allowed a 15-minute break every 4 hours. These breaks will be paid. In addition, all employees who work at least 8 hours in a day are entitled to take a 60-minute meal break. Meal breaks are generally unpaid.

However, employees who are required to work or remain at their stations during the meal break will be paid for that time.

Employees need to clock-in and clock-out for lunch breaks. 15-minutes breaks are scheduled and monitored by the shift supervisor.

OVERTIME

On occasion, we may ask employees to work beyond their regular scheduled hours. We expect employees to work a reasonable amount of overtime as a job requirement.

We will try to give employees advance notice when overtime work is necessary; however, advance notice will not always be possible.

Exempt employees will not be paid for working beyond their regular scheduled hours. Nonexempt employees are entitled to payment for overtime, according to the rules set forth below.

All overtime work must be approved in writing, in advance, by the employee's supervisor. Working overtime without permission violates company policy and may result in disciplinary action.

For purposes of calculating how many hours an employee has worked in a day or week, our work week begins at 12:01 a.m. on Monday and ends at midnight on Sunday. Our workday begins at 12:01 a.m. and ends at midnight each day.

Nonexempt employees will be paid 1.5 times their regular hourly rate of pay for every hour worked in excess of 40 hours.

Here are some optional policies on bulletin board use you may choose to adopt instead of the example above:

- *Only time actually spent working counts as hours worked. Vacation time, sick days, holidays, or any other paid time during which an employee did not actually work will not count as hours worked.*

- *Hours worked means all time spent actually working, plus _____.*

- *The company will pay employees a premium for working on the following holidays: _____. Employees who agree to work on these days will receive _____.*

- *Please let your supervisor know if you wish to work overtime. Your supervisor will add your name to the overtime list. When overtime is available, it will be offered first to employees on the list in the order in which their names appear. If overtime work is necessary and no employees on the list are available, employees who are eligible to perform the work—that is, employees who do the same type of work during their regular work hours—will be asked to work overtime, in alphabetical order. After an employee, on the list or off, has worked overtime, the next employee on the list or in alphabetical order will be asked to work overtime when it next becomes available, and so on.*

PAY POLICIES

LANE'S GARDEN

FLORAL & GIFTS

PAYDAY

Employees are paid every week. You will receive your paycheck on Friday. If a payday falls on a holiday, you will receive your paycheck on the last workday immediately before that payday.

Employees must submit their time cards or time sheets to their supervisor three before payday.

ADVANCE POLICY *(side tab)*

ADVANCE POLICY

Please submit requests for pay advances to Mary Vandercless. Requests will be granted or denied at the sole discretion of the company.

If we grant your request for an advance, you may receive no more than 2 weeks pay advance.

Here are some optional policies on pay advances:

- *Our company does not allow employees to receive pay advances.*

- *An employee who will be on vacation or other paid leave on payday may request an early paycheck. Please submit these requests to the payroll administrator. We will do our best to accommodate your request within the time allowed.*

- *All advances must be repaid within _____ days. Your request for an additional advance will be denied automatically if you have not yet repaid a previous advance.*

- *All advances must be paid back, through payroll deductions, within _____ days. Your request for an additional advance will be denied automatically if you have not yet repaid a previous advance.*

- *An employee who will be on vacation or other paid leave on payday may request an early paycheck. Please submit these requests to the payroll administrator. Although we cannot guarantee that every request will be granted, we will do our best to accommodate your request.*

TIP CREDIT

Employees who hold certain positions in our company receive some of their compensation in the form of tips from customers. If you receive tips, the company will pay you an hourly wage of at least $5.15. However, if your wage and tips you actually earn during any pay period do not add up to at least the minimum wage for every hour you work, the company will pay you the difference.

TIP POOLING

Delivery employees in the following positions are required to pool tips. If you are a delivery person, you must contribute 50 percent of your tips to the pool at the end of each workday. The pool will be divided equally among all employees who worked that day.

TIPS

PAYROLL DEDUCTIONS

Your paycheck reflects your total earnings for the pay period, as well as any mandatory or voluntary deductions from your paycheck. Mandatory deductions are defined as those we are legally required to take, such as federal income tax, social security tax (FICA), and any applicable state taxes. Voluntary deductions are deductions that you have authorized. If you have any questions about your deductions, or wish to change your federal withholding form (Form W-4), contact Mary Vandercless.

WAGE GARNISHMENTS

A wage garnishment is a court order directing us to withhold a set amount of money from an employee's paycheck and send to a person or agency. Wages can be garnished to pay child support, spousal support, tax debts, outstanding student loans, or money owed because of a judgment in a civil lawsuit.

If we are instructed to garnish an employee's wages, the employee will be notified of the garnishment at once. We are legally required to comply with these orders. If you dispute the amount, you must contact the court or agency that issued the order.

EXPENSE REIMBURSEMENT

Employees may incur expenses on behalf of Lane's Garden. We will reimburse you for the actual work-related expenses you incur as long as those expenses are reasonable. You must follow these procedures to be reimbursed:

- Get permission from your supervisor before incurring an expense.

- The company maintains a list of preferred vendors for various work-related items and services. You must use these vendors, if possible. You can get a current copy of the list from Mary Vandercless.

- Keep a receipt or some other proof of payment for every expense.

- Submit your receipts, along with an expense report, to your supervisor for approval within 30 days of incurring an expense.

- Your supervisor is responsible for submitting your expense report to Mary Vandercless. If your report is approved, you will receive your reimbursement with your next paycheck.

Remember that you are spending the company's money when you pay for business-related expenses. We expect you to save money wherever possible. Your supervisor can assist you in deciding whether an expense is appropriate.

EXPENSE REIMBURSEMENT

PROCEDURES FOR TRAVEL EXPENSES

If employees are required to travel for work, the company will reimburse you for your travel expenses, including:

- the cost of travel to and from the airport or train station, including parking expenses and tolls

- the cost of airline or train tickets – such tickets must be coach class if possible

- the cost of an economy class rental car, if necessary

- a mileage reimbursement for those employees who prefer to use their own cars for company travel

- the cost of lodging—employees should select moderately priced lodging if possible, and the cost of meals and other incidental expenses, up to a per diem of $200

You must request advance approval of all travel expenses from your supervisor and follow the procedures above to have your expenses reimbursed.

MILEAGE REIMBURSEMENT

Employees who use their own vehicle for company business will be reimbursed at the rate of $0.10 per mile. Employees are not entitled to separate reimbursement for gas, maintenance, insurance, or other vehicle-related expenses; the reimbursement rate above is intended to encompass all of these expenses.

Before using a personal vehicle for work-related purposes, employees must demonstrate that they have a valid driver's license and adequate insurance coverage. The company does not reimburse employees for their commute to and from the workplace.

To claim mileage reimbursement, you must follow these procedures:

Keep a written record of your business-related travel, including the total mileage of each business trip, the date of travel, destination, and the purpose of your trip.

If you anticipate having to travel an unusually long distance, get your supervisor's approval before making the trip.

Submit your record to your supervisor for approval on the last day of the month.

Your supervisor is responsible for submitting your record to Mary Vandercless. If your record is approved, you will receive your reimbursement payment with your next paycheck.

MILEAGE REIMBURSEMENT

EMPLOYEE BENEFITS

As part of our commitment to our employees and their well-being, Lane's Garden provides employees with a variety of benefit plans:

- Medical/Life Insurance
- Retirement Plan
- Paid Holidays
- Paid Vacation
- Sick Leave

Although we introduce you to those plans in this section, we cannot provide the details of each plan here. You should receive official plan documents for each of the benefit plans that we offer. Those documents (along with any updates that we give to you) should be your primary resource for information about your benefit plans. If you see any conflict between those documents and the information in this handbook, the official plan documents should be relied upon.

The benefits we provide are meant to help employees maintain a high quality of life—both professionally and personally. We sincerely hope that each employee will take full advantage of these benefits. If you do not understand information in the plan documents or if you have any questions about the benefits we offer, please talk to Mary Vandercless.

MEDICAL INSURANCE

EMPLOYEE BENEFITS

All full-time employees are eligible for health insurance through the Liberty Medical Plan.

If you enroll, Lane's Garden will pay some of the cost of your coverage under the Liberty Medical Plan. You may purchase coverage for qualified dependents by payroll deduction. Premiums are deducted from your paycheck and are tax-sheltered unless you elect otherwise.

If you are employed on a regular part-time basis for half-time or more, you may participate in the group plan by paying the entire cost.

Our plan is traditional coverage, in which you receive medical care from any doctor. You pay a deductible toward your medical expenses each year before the plan pays anything. You then pay a percentage of any further costs up to a maximum amount each year, and the plan pays the rest. There are additional co-payments for drugs, office visits, for use of a hospital which is not a Preferred Provider, and for hospital admission which do not count in your yearly deductible.

See the Liberty Medical Plan package for full details.

Note: Because the text of all benefits depend on the specifics of your company and state laws, we cannot provide you with a standard policy to use. The above is only an example. Please see the main discussion for assistance in drafting this policy language yourself.

LIFE INSURANCE

After 90 days of employment, regular full-time and part-time employees are eligible for paid life insurance coverage. Through age 65 the insurance coverage is equal to 1.5 times the amount of an employee's base annual salary. Over age 65, the amount of insurance is equal to 1 times the base annual salary. In addition, optional insurance is available to employees at low group rates. The maximum amount of insurance is $500,000, for basic term life and optional life combined. An employee leaving Lane's Garden may convert this insurance to a private non-group plan within 60 days and continue it at his or her own expense. To do so, he or she must contact Mary Vandercless.

RETIREMENT PLAN

Lane's Garden Retirement Plan is a 401(k) defined contribution plan provided through individual annuity or investment contracts.

All regular full-time and part-time employees over age 21 can voluntarily participate in the Plan after two years of employment. The employee may elect to make contributions on a before-tax or after-tax basis. All contributions and earnings on investments are tax sheltered until benefits are received. Employees direct the investment of these contributions by working with Lane's Garden financial analyst Katie May Heldt. The employee immediately and fully owns all contributions to the Plan; there is no vesting period.

For specific plan information, please refer to the Summary Plan Description for the or contact Mary Vandercless.

EMPLOYEE BENEFITS

PAID HOLIDAYS

Lane's Garden officially closes for three holidays throughout the year. All regular full-time employees are eligible for holiday pay based on their straight-time hourly rate. The holidays are:

- Thanksgiving Day
- Christmas Day
- New Year's Day

When a holiday falls on a Sunday, the following Monday will be observed as the paid holiday. If the holiday falls on a Saturday, the preceding Friday will be observed. A holiday schedule is distributed at the beginning of each year.

Here is an alternative to allow floating holidays:

- *Eligible employees are also entitled to take ____ floating holidays each year. These holidays may be used to observe a religious holiday, to celebrate your birthday, or to take a day off for personal reasons. You must schedule your floating holidays with your supervisor in advance. If you do not use your floating holidays during the year, you may not carry them over to the next year.*

PAID VACATION

Lane's Garden believes employees deserve periods of rest from their duties and responsibilities. All regular full-time employees are eligible for paid vacation leave.

Vacation is earned based on years of service. Vacation time must be used within the calendar year in which it is earned and cannot be carried over to the next year without the written consent of Mary Vandercless.

Vacation for full-time employees is earned as follows:

- 1 year of service = 1 week
- 2 years of service = 2 weeks
- 5 years of service = 3 weeks
- 10 years of service = 4 weeks

Employees are encouraged to cooperate with each other in arranging for vacation leave, recognizing that there may be minimum coverage requirements necessitating the scheduling of vacation leave at certain periods of time. Requests for vacation leave are subject to the approval of the supervisor and should be made as far in advance as possible.

EMPLOYEE BENEFITS

Here are a number of alternative vacation policies:

- *Our company recognizes that our employees need to take time off occasionally to rest and relax, to enjoy a vacation, or to attend to personal matters. That is why we offer a paid vacation program. _____ employees are eligible to participate in the paid vacation program. Eligible employees accrue vacation time according to the following schedule: [Insert schedule here]. Employees must schedule their vacations in advance with their supervisor. We will try to grant every employee's vacation request for their choice of days off. However, we must have enough workers to meet our day-to-day needs, meaning we might not be able to grant every vacation request, especially during holiday periods.*

- *Employees may not accrue more than _____ of vacation time. When an employee's vacation balance reaches this limit, an employee may accrue more vacation only by taking some vacation time to bring the employee's balance back below the limit.*

- *Employees will be paid for any accrued and unused vacation when their employment terminates.*

SICK LEAVE

Lane's Garden provides paid sick days to full time employees. Eligible employees accrue 6 sick days per year at the rate of .5 per month. The company will not pay employees for sick days that have accrued but have not been used by the time employment ends.

Employees may use sick leave when they are unable to work because of illness or injury. Sick leave is not to be used as extra vacation time or personal days. Any employee who abuses sick leave may be subject to discipline.

We ask that employees call in as soon as they realize that they will be unable to work before the regular start of their work day. You must report to your supervisor by phone each day you are out on leave.

EMPLOYEE BENEFITS

Here are some sick leave alternatives:

- *Employees may accrue a maximum of _____ of sick leave. When an employee has reached this limit, no more sick leave will accrue until the employee uses sick leave to reduce the accrued total below the maximum.*

- *Employees may also use sick leave to _____.*

Alternative to Vacation and Sick Leave: PTO

Paid Time Off (PTO) is a popular alternative to vacations and sick leave. If you choose to offer this, here are some policies you may want to adapt:

- *Instead of offering separate vacation, sick leave, and personal days or floating holidays, (insert company name) offers a paid time off ("PTO") program that combines all of these benefits. We believe this program will give employees the flexibility to manage their time off as they see fit. Employees may use PTO for sickness, vacation, to attend a child's school activities, to care for elderly or ill family members, to take care of personal errands or business, or simply to take a day off work.*

  You are eligible to participate in the PTO program if you _____. (For information on employee classifications, see Section __ of this handbook.) PTO accrues according to the following schedule: (insert schedule).

  Employees must schedule time off in advance with their supervisors. We will try to grant every employee's PTO request for the days off they choose. However, we must have enough workers to meet our day-to-day needs, meaning we might not be able to grant every PTO request, especially during holiday or seasonally busy periods.

  If circumstances, such as a medical or family emergency, prevent advance scheduling, you must inform your supervisor as soon as possible that you are taking paid time off.

Because PTO encompasses vacation and sick leave, employees must manage their PTO responsibly to ensure that they have time available for emergencies, such as personal or family illness. An employee who needs time off but has no accrued PTO may be eligible to take unpaid leave. The company will decide these requests on a case-by-case basis.

Employees may not accrue more than _____ of PTO. When an employee's PTO balance reaches this limit, an employee may accrue more PTO only by taking some PTO to bring the employee's balance back below the limit.

Employees will be paid for any accrued and unused PTO when their employment ends.

FAMILY AND MEDICAL LEAVE

Employees who have worked for our company for at least a full year and have worked an average of at least 25 hours per week are eligible to take unpaid family and medical leave for these purposes:

- because the employee's own serious health condition makes the employee unable to work

- to care for a spouse, child, or parent who has a serious health condition, or

- to care for a newborn, newly adopted child, or recently placed foster child.

LEAVE AVAILABLE

Eligible employees may take up to 12 weeks of unpaid leave per calendar year for any of the above purposes. For purposes of calculating available family and medical leave, the year starts on January 1.

A parent who takes leave to care for a newborn, newly adopted child, or recently placed foster child must begin this leave within a year after the birth, adoption, or placement.

NOTICE REQUIREMENTS

Employees are required to give at least 30 days notice of their need for family and medical leave, if their need is foreseeable. In emergencies and unexpected situations, employees must give as much notice as is practicable under the circumstances.

REINSTATEMENT RIGHTS

When you return from an approved family and medical leave, you have the right to return to your former position or an equivalent position, except:

You have no greater right to reinstatement than you would have had if you had not been on leave. If your position is eliminated for reasons unrelated to your leave, for example, you have no right to reinstatement.

Lane's Garden is not obligated to reinstate you if you are a key employee —that is, you are among the highest-paid 10 percent of our workforce and holding your job open during your leave would cause the company substantial economic harm. If the company classifies you as a key employee under this definition, you will be notified when you request leave.

MEDICAL CERTIFICATION

Lane's Garden may ask employees who take leave for their own serious health condition or to care for a spouse, parent, or child with a serious health condition to provide a doctor's form certifying the need for leave. The company is also entitled to seek a second opinion and periodic recertification. In some cases, the company may ask employees who take leave because of their own serious health condition to provide a fitness-for-duty report from their doctors before they return to work.

FAMILY AND MEDICAL LEAVE

INTERMITTENT LEAVE

If you will need to take family and medical leave on an intermittent basis—that is, a day or two at a time rather than all at once—for your own serious health condition or to take care of a family member with a serious health condition, you will be allowed to do so. However, the company may temporarily reassign you to a different position with equivalent pay and benefits to accommodate the intermittent schedule.

The company will consider requests for intermittent leave to care for a new child on a case-by-case basis.

HEALTH INSURANCE DURING LEAVE

Your health insurance benefits will continue during leave. You will be responsible for paying any portion of the premium that you ordinarily pay while you are working, and you must make arrangements to make these payments while you are out. Employees who do not return from family and medical leave may be required to reimburse the company for any premiums paid on the employee's behalf during the leave.

Here are some alternatives for Family and Medical Leave:

- *Because of our small size, our company is not required to comply with the federal Family and Medical Leave Act (FMLA). However, we recognize that our employees may occasionally need to take unpaid leave to care for a new child, to care for a seriously ill family member, or to handle an employee's own medical issues. If you anticipate that you might need time off to deal with family and medical issues, please talk to your supervisor. We cannot guarantee that we will grant every request, but we will seriously consider every request on a case-by-case basis. Among other things, we may consider our staffing needs, your position at the company, the reason that you need leave, and how long you expect your leave to last.*

- *An employee who has accrued paid time off (select one: must/ may) use these benefits to receive pay for all or a portion of family and medical leave.*

BEREAVEMENT LEAVE

In the event of the death of an immediate family member, you are entitled to take up to 14 days off work. This leave will be paid. Additional time off can be taken on an unpaid basis and will be approved on a case-by-case basis.

Immediate family members include:

- Parent
- Spouse or Life Partner
- Child
- Sibling

The company will consider, on a case-by-case basis, requests for bereavement leave for the death of someone who does not qualify as an immediate family member under this policy.

BEREAVEMENT LEAVE

MILITARY LEAVE

Lane's Garden supports those who serve in the U.S. armed forces. In keeping with this commitment and in accordance with state and federal law, employees who must be absent from work for military service are entitled to take a military leave of absence. This leave will be unpaid.

When an employee's military leave ends, that employee will be reinstated to the position he or she formerly held or to a comparable position as long as the employee meets the requirements of federal and state law.

Employees who are called to military service must tell their supervisors as soon as possible that they will need to take military leave. An employee whose military service has ended must return to work or inform the company that he or she wants to be reinstated in accordance with these guidelines:

For a leave of 30 or fewer days, the employee must report back to work on the first regularly scheduled workday after completing military service, allowing for travel time For a leave of 31 to 180 days, the employee must request reinstatement within 14 days after military service ends For a leave of 181 days or more, the employee must request reinstatement within 90 days after military service ends.

MILITARY LEAVE

Here are some military leave alternatives clauses:

- *During this unpaid leave, employees are entitled to use applicable paid time off (vacation time or personal days).*

- *The company will continue your health insurance benefits during your leave under these circumstances: If you are absent for 30 or fewer days, you will be treated as any employee not on leave. The company will continue to pay its share of the insurance premium, and you must continue to pay your usual share. If your leave lasts longer than 30 days, you will have to pay the entire premium to continue your benefits.*

DISABILITY INSURANCE

STATE DISABILITY INSURANCE

Sometimes an employee suffers an illness or injury outside of the workplace that prevents the employee from working and earning income. If this happens to you, state disability insurance may provide you with a percentage of your salary while you are unable to work. All employees are eligible for this coverage and pay for it through deductions from their paychecks.

If you suffer from a work-related illness or injury, you may be eligible for worker's compensation insurance instead of state disability insurance. See the Worker's Compensation policy, below. To find out more about state disability insurance, contact Mary Vandercless.

UNEMPLOYMENT INSURANCE

If your employment with our company ends, you may be eligible for unemployment benefits. These benefits provide you with a percentage of your wages while you are unemployed and looking for work. To find out more, contact Mary Vandercless.

WORKERS' COMPENSATION INSURANCE

If you suffer from a work-related illness or injury, you may be eligible for workers' compensation benefits which pay for medical care and lost wages resulting from job-related illnesses or injuries. If you are injured or become ill through work, please inform your supervisor immediately regardless of how minor the injury or illness might be. To find out more about worker's compensation coverage, contact Mary Vandercless.

COMPANY PROPERTY

We have invested a great deal of money in the property and equipment that you use to perform your job. It is a senseless and avoidable drain on this company's bottom line when people abuse company property, misuse it, or wear it out prematurely by using it for personal business.

We ask all employees to take care of company property and to report any problems to Mary Vandercless. If a piece of equipment or property is unsafe for use, please report it immediately. Please use property only in the manner intended and as instructed. We do not allow personal use of company property unless specifically authorized in this handbook.

Failure to use company property appropriately and failure to report problems or unsafe conditions may result in disciplinary action, up to and including discharge.

RETURN OF COMPANY PROPERTY

When your employment with this company ends, we expect you to return company property—clean and in good repair. This includes this employee handbook, all manuals and guides, documents, phones, computers, equipment, keys, and tools. We reserve the right to take any lawful action to recover or protect our property.

If you do not return a piece of property, we will withhold from your final paycheck the cost of replacing that piece of property. If you return a piece of property in disrepair, we will withhold from your final paycheck the cost of repair. We also reserve the right to take any other lawful action necessary to recover or protect our property.

COMPANY CARS

We have invested in company vehicles so that our employees can use them on deliveries and other company business in place of their own vehicles.

We need your help in keeping company cars in the best condition possible. Please keep them clean and remove any trash or personal items when you are finished using the vehicles.

Please immediately report any accidents, mechanical problems, or other problems to Mary Vandercless. We will try to have company vehicles repaired or serviced as soon as possible.

Only authorized employees may use company cars, and they may do so only on company business. You may not use company vehicles while under the influence of drugs or alcohol or while otherwise impaired.

You must have a valid driver's license to use company cars, and we expect that you will drive in a safe and courteous manner. If you receive any tickets for parking violations or moving violations, you are responsible for taking care of them.

Violating this policy in any way may result in disciplinary action, up to and including discharge.

COMPANY CARS

COMPANY CARS

If you have been assigned a company car, it is your responsibility to keep the car in good condition and repair. At a minimum, this means keeping the car clean and bringing it in for scheduled maintenance by an authorized service department. Periodically, we may inform you of other ways you must care for the car. We will, of course, reimburse you for any ordinary expenses associated with maintaining the vehicle.

Here is an alternative company car clause regarding accidents:

- *If you are involved in an accident while driving a (name of company) vehicle, your first concern should be for the welfare of passengers or pedestrians. You should seek first aid assistance and/or an ambulance for injured passengers*

  The following procedures should be followed in the event of an accident involving a company vehicle:

  If the vehicle needs to be towed, call (name of person or department and phone number).

  Notify your manager/supervisor.

  Arrange to receive a copy of the accident report filed by the police authorities.

  Fill out an (name of form) and turn it in (name of department or person).

TELEPHONE SYSTEM

TELEPHONE SYSTEM

The company's telephone system is for business use only. Employees are expected to keep personal calls to a minimum. If you must make or receive a personal call, please keep your conversation brief. Extensive personal use of company phones is grounds for discipline.

VOTING

VOTING

Our company encourages employees to exercise their right to vote. If your work schedule and the location of your polling place will make it difficult for you to get to the polls before they close, you are entitled to take up to 1 hour off work at the beginning or end of your shift to cast your ballot. This time will be unpaid. Employees who will need to take time off work to vote must inform their supervisors at least 1 day in advance. Employees are expected to work with their supervisors to ensure that their absence does not negatively affect company operations.

JURY DUTY

If you are called for jury duty, you are entitled to take time off, as necessary, to fulfill your jury obligations. This leave will be unpaid. No employee will face discipline or retaliation for jury service.

You must immediately inform your supervisor when you receive your jury duty summons. If you are chosen to sit on a jury, you must inform your supervisor how long the trial is expected to last. You must also check in with your supervisor periodically during your jury service, so the company knows when to expect you back at work.

Here is are some alternative jury duty clauses:

- *You will be paid for up to ____ days of jury service; if your service extends beyond this period, the remainder of your leave will be unpaid.*

- *On any day when your jury service ends before the end of your usual work day, you must check in with your supervisor to find out whether you need to return to work for that day.*

JOB PERFORMANCE

JOB PERFORMANCE

Each employee at Lane's Garden contributes to the success or failure of our company. If one employee allows his or her performance to slip, then all of us suffer. We expect everyone to perform to the highest level possible.

Poor job performance can lead to discipline, up to and including discharge.

PERFORMANCE REVIEWS

Because our employees' performance is vital to our success, we conduct periodic reviews of individual employee performance. We hope that, through these reviews, our employees will learn what we expect of them, and we will learn what they expect of us.

We require all employees to participate in the review process. Failure to participate could lead to discipline, up to and including discharge. To learn more about our performance review system, contact Mary Vandercless.

Because the text of this modification depends on the specifics of your company and state law, we cannot provide you with standard language to use. Please see the main discussion for assistance in drafting this modification language yourself.

WORKPLACE BEHAVIOR

People who work together have an impact on each other's performance, productivity, and personal satisfaction in their jobs. In addition, how our employees act toward customers and vendors will influence whether those relationships are successful for our company.

Because your conduct affects many other people, we expect you to act in a professional manner whenever you are on company property, conducting company business, or representing the company at business or social functions.

Although it is impossible to give an exhaustive list of everything that professional conduct means, at a minimum it includes the following:

- following all of the rules in this handbook that apply to you
- refraining from rude, offensive, or outrageous behavior
- refraining from ridicule and hostile jokes
- treating coworkers, customers, and vendors with patience, respect, and consideration
- being courteous and helpful to others, and
- communicating openly with supervisors, managers, and coworkers.

Individuals who act unprofessionally will face discipline, up to and including discharge.

WORKPLACE BEHAVIOR

SERVING CUSTOMERS

The success of this company depends in great part on the loyalty and good will of our customers. As a result, we expect our employees to behave in the following manner when interacting with customers:

- to treat all customers with courtesy and respect
- to be helpful and cheerful toward customers
- to attend to customers as quickly as possible above all other duties

PUNCTUALITY AND ATTENDANCE

You are important to the effective operation of this business. When you are not here at expected times or on expected days, someone else must do your job or delay doing his or her own job while waiting for you to arrive. If you work with customers or vendors, they may grow frustrated if they cannot reach you during your scheduled work times.

As a result, we expect you to keep regular attendance and to be on time and ready to work at the beginning of each scheduled workday.

Of course, things will sometimes happen to prevent you from getting to work on time. For example, you may be delayed by weather, a sick child, or car trouble. If you are going to be more than 15 minutes late, please call Lane's Garden main office at 608-788-5263). If you cannot reach the office, please contact Mary Vandercless. Please give this notice as far in advance as possible.

WORKPLACE BEHAVIOR

If you must miss a full day of work for reasons other than vacation, sick leave, or other approved leave (such as leave to serve on a jury or for a death in a family), you must notify your supervisor as far in advance as possible. If you cannot reach this person, contact Mary Vandercless.

If you are late for work or fail to appear or notify the company as required by this policy or by other policies in this handbook, you will face disciplinary action, up to and including discharge.

EMPLOYEE APPEARANCE & DRESS

We ask all employees to use common sense when they dress for work. Please dress appropriately for your position and job duties and make sure you are neat and clean at all times.

If you have any questions about the proper attire for your position, please contact your supervisor. We will try to accommodate an employee's special dress or grooming needs that are the result of religion, ethnicity, race, or disability.

WORKPLACE BEHAVIOR

Here are some alternative clauses regarding appearance:

- *Employees must wear a uniform during work hours. Please make sure you are neat and clean at all times, and please keep your uniform clean and in good condition. If you have any questions about your uniform or about our appearance standards, please contact (insert name of person).*

- *We place specific restrictions on the dress and appearance of some employees for safety reasons. To learn about those restrictions, refer to _____.*

- *We believe that a professional image enhances our work product and makes us more competitive in the marketplace. That image is conveyed in part through the appearance of our employees. We ask all employees to use their common sense when dressing for work and to wear professional and appropriate attire. We also ask our employees to maintain a neat and clean appearance at all times.*

- *Although we do require professional attire Monday through Thursday, we celebrate Fridays here by allowing employees to dress casually. Acceptable casual clothing includes (list acceptable types of clothing). Unacceptable casual clothing includes (list acceptable types of clothing). Even on Fridays, however, we ask employees to use good judgment and to maintain a neat and clean appearance.*

PRANKS AND PRACTICAL JOKES

Although we want our employees to enjoy their jobs and have fun working together, we cannot allow employees to play practical jokes or pranks on each other. At best, these actions disrupt the workplace and dampen the morale of some; at worst, they lead to complaints of discrimination, harassment, or assault. Employees who play pranks or practical jokes will face disciplinary action, up to and including discharge. If you have any questions about this policy, contact Mary Vandercless.

HORSEPLAY

Although we want our employees to have fun while they work, we do not allow employees to engage in horseplay which disrupts the work environment and can get out of hand, leading to fighting, hurt feelings, safety hazards, or worse.

Employees who engage in horseplay will face disciplinary action, up to and including discharge.

FIGHTING

Verbal or physical fighting among employees is absolutely prohibited. Employees shall not engage in, provoke, or encourage a fight. Those who violate this policy will be disciplined, up to and including discharge.

WORKPLACE BEHAVIOR

WORKPLACE BEHAVIOR

THREATENING, ABUSIVE, OR VULGAR LANGUAGE

We expect our employees to treat everyone they meet through their jobs with courtesy and respect. Threatening, abusive, and vulgar language has no place at this company. It destroys morale and relationships, and it impedes the effective and efficient operation of our business.

As a result, we will not tolerate threatening, abusive, or vulgar language from employees while they are on the work site, conducting company business, or attending company-related business or social functions.

If you have any questions about this policy, contact Mary Vandercless.

Employees who violate this policy will face disciplinary action, up to and including discharge.

SLEEPING ON THE JOB

When our employees arrive at work, we expect them to be physically prepared to work through their day. Employees who sleep on the job dampen morale and productivity and deprive us of their work and companionship.

For certain employees, sleeping on the job creates a safety hazard. Employees who do deliveries create unacceptable risks to their own safety and the safety of others when they fail to be attentive and alert while working. For these employees, sleeping on the job violates both this policy and our safety policies.

As a result, we do not allow any employees to sleep while at work. Employees who feel sick or unable to finish the day because of weariness should talk to insert name of person) about using sick leave to take the rest of the day off.

INSUBORDINATION

This workplace operates on a system of mutual respect between supervisors and employees. Supervisors must treat their employees with dignity and understanding, and employees must show due regard for their supervisors' authority.

Insubordination occurs when employees unreasonably refuse to obey the orders or follow the instructions of their supervisors. It also occurs when employees, through their actions or words, show disrespect toward their supervisors.

Insubordinate employees will face discipline, up to and including discharge.

We understand, however, that there will be times when employees have valid reasons for refusing to do as their supervisor says. Perhaps the employee fears for his safety or the safety of others. Perhaps the employee believes that following instructions will violate the law or pose some other problem for this company. Or maybe the employee thinks that there is a better way to accomplish a goal or perform a task. When these issues arise, we do not ask that employees blindly follow orders. Instead, we ask that employees explain the situation to their supervisor. If, after hearing the employee's side, the supervisor continues to give the same order or rule, the employee must either obey or use the complaint procedures described in later in this handbook.

WORKPLACE BEHAVIOR

PROGRESSIVE DISCIPLINE

Here are the progressive discipline steps taken for non-exempt employees that have completed the probationary period:

- The supervisor discusses with the employee the specific performance problem, what improvements are needed, and a date by which corrections should occur. The supervisor will document the date and content of the conversation. No official notation will go into the employee's file at this time.

- If the performance problem persists, the supervisor and the employee will have another discussion. A written warning will be issued to the employee. This warning will contain a statement of the problem, what corrections are necessary, and a date by which the improvement should occur. The employee will be asked to sign the form indicating she or he has read it. A copy will be placed in the employee's personnel file, and a copy will be given to the employee.

- If the performance problem still persists, a second written warning will be issued.

- If the performance problem recurs after the second written warning, disciplinary action (including discharge) may occur.

Written warnings are removed from the employee's file after one year of employment if there have been no subsequent warnings.

WORKPLACE BEHAVIOR

Because the text of a discipline policy depends on the specifics of your company and state law, we cannot provide you with a standard policy to use. Please see the main discussion for assistance in drafting this policy language yourself.

SAFETY POLICY

Lane's Garden takes employee safety seriously. To provide a safe workplace for everyone, every employee must follow our safety rules:

Employees must follow their supervisors' safety instructions.

Employees in certain positions may be required to wear protective equipment, such as hair nets, hard hats, safety glasses, work boots, ear plugs, or masks. Your supervisor will let you know if your position requires protective gear.

Employees in certain positions may be prohibited from wearing dangling jewelry or apparel, or may be required to pull back or cover their hair for safety purposes. Your supervisor will tell you if you fall into one of these categories.

All equipment and machinery must be used properly. This means all guards, restraints, and other safety devices must be used at all times. Do not use equipment for other than its intended purpose.

All employees must immediately report any workplace condition that they believe to be unsafe to their supervisor. The company will look into the matter promptly.

All employees must immediately report any workplace accident or injury to his or her immediate supervisor.

HEALTH & SAFETY

You may want to add specific safety instructions pertaining to your industry or equipment. Because the text of this modification depends on the specifics of your company and state law, we cannot provide you with standard language to use. Please see the main discussion for assistance in drafting this policy language yourself.

WORKPLACE SECURITY

It is every employee's responsibility to help keep our workplace secure from unauthorized intruders. Every employee must comply with these security precautions.

When you leave work for the day, please make sure to follow the lock-up procedure checklist posted in the employee breakroom.

After-hours access to the workplace is limited to those employees who need to work late. If you are going to be working past our usual closing time, please let your supervisor know.

Employees are allowed to have an occasional visitor in the workplace, but workplace visits should be the exception rather than the rule. If you are anticipating a visitor, please let your supervisor know. When your visitor arrives, you will be notified.

HEALTH & SAFETY

Here are some alternative clauses regarding visitors and security:

- *Visitors must wear an identification badge at all times when they are in our workplace. Visitors can get a badge at _____. They must return the badge when they leave company premises.*

- *Do not leave your visitor unattended in the workplace. If you have a visitor, you must accompany your visitor at all times. This includes escorting your visitor to and from the entrance to our company.*

- *If you are the last to leave the workplace for the evening, you are responsible for doing all of the following: _____. If you have questions about any of these responsibilities, please talk to your supervisor.*

WHAT TO DO IN AN EMERGENCY

If you observe a fire, emergency, serious incident or threat of violence IMMEDIATELY DIAL 911 and report it. If the incident or threat does not appear to require immediate police, fire or medical intervention, please contact Mary Vandercless and report it as soon as possible, using the company's complaint procedure. All complaints will be investigated and appropriate action will be taken. You will not face retaliation for making a complaint.

HEALTH & SAFETY

Here are some alternative clauses regarding visitors and security:

- *In case of an emergency such as a fire or accident, your first priority should be your own safety. In the event of an emergency causing serious injuries, IMMEDIATELY DIAL 911 to alert police and rescue workers of the situation. If you hear a fire alarm or in case of an emergency that requires evacuation, please proceed quickly and calmly to the fire exits. The company will hold periodic fire drills to familiarize everyone with the routes they should take. Remember that every second may count—do not return to the workplace to retrieve personal belongings or work-related items. After you have exited the building, head towards the _____ _____.*

- *(Insert company name) keeps emergency supplies on hand. First aid kits are located _____. Fire extinguishers can be found _____. Earthquake preparedness kits are kept _____ _____. We also keep a supply of flashlights in _____.*

LANE'S GARDEN
FLORAL & GIFTS

SMOKING POLICY

SMOKING POLICY

To accommodate employees who smoke as well as those who do not, the company has created smoking and nonsmoking areas. Smoking is allowed only in the employee smoking breakroom, located to the left of the walk-in cooler.

The company has posted signs designating smoking and nonsmoking areas. Employees who smoke are required to observe these signs and to smoke in designated areas only.

Your company may not allow smoking, or offer insurance programs to help employees quit. Here are some alternative smoking clauses:

- *For the health, comfort, and safety of our employees, smoking is not allowed on company property.*

- *You may smoke during meal or rest breaks only. Employees may not take "smoking breaks" in addition to the regular breaks provided to every employee under our policies.*

- *Our company encourages those who wish to quit smoking. Our health insurance provider offers a program to help employees stop smoking. If you are interested in this program, ask _____*

_____ *for more details, or you can contact our insurance carrier directly.*

- *Our company encourages those who wish to quit smoking. If you are interested in participating in getting help to stop smoking, the _____ can direct you to local smoking cessation programs. If you complete one of the programs on the company's approved list, we will pay the cost of your participation.*

- *We recognize that smoking tobacco products is legal and that employees have the right to smoke outside of work hours. (Company name) will not discriminate against any applicant or employee based on that person's choice to smoke.*

- *You may smoke during meal or rest breaks only. Employees may not take "smoking breaks" in addition to the regular breaks provided to every employee under our policies.*

WORKPLACE VIOLENCE

We will not tolerate violence in the workplace. Violence includes physical altercations, coercion, pushing or shoving, horseplay, intimidation, stalking, and threats of violence. Any comments about violence will be taken seriously—and may result in your discharge. Please do not joke or make offhand remarks about violence.

NO WEAPONS

No weapons are allowed in our workplace. Weapons include firearms, knives, brass knuckles, martial arts equipment, clubs or bats, and explosives. If your work requires you to use an item that might qualify as a weapon, you must receive authorization from your supervisor to bring that item to work or use it in the workplace. Any employee found with an unauthorized weapon in the workplace will be subject to discipline, up to and including discharge.

WHAT TO DO IN CASE OF VIOLENCE

If you observe a serious incident or threat of violence IMMEDIATELY DIAL 911 and report it to the police. If the incident or threat does not appear to require immediate police intervention, please contact Mary Vandercless and report it as soon as possible, using the company's complaint procedure. All complaints will be investigated and appropriate action will be taken. You will not face retaliation for making a complaint.

WORKPLACE VIOLENCE

Here are some alternative clauses if your company allows weapons:

- *Weapons are generally not allowed in our workplace. Weapons include firearms, knives, brass knuckles, martial arts equipment, clubs or bats, and explosives. However, some of our employees are required to carry weapons to perform their jobs. Weapons may be required in the following positions: _____. If you hold one of these positions, ask your supervisor whether you will be required to carry a weapon. If your job requires you to carry a weapon, you must receive authorization from your supervisor to do so. You may be required to complete training courses, pass a safety test, and get a license to be authorized to carry a weapon.*

- *If you observe a serious incident or threat of violence, call security personnel _____ at _____. If you are unable to reach someone at this number, IMMEDIATELY DIAL 911 and report the incident to the police. If the incident or threat does not appear to require immediate police intervention, please contact _____ and report it as soon as possible, using the company's complaint procedure. All complaints will be investigated and appropriate action will be taken. You will not face retaliation for making a complaint.*

LANE'S GARDEN

FLORAL & GIFTS

EMPLOYEE PRIVACY

Employees do not have a right to privacy in their work spaces, any other company property, or any personal property they bring to the workplace. The company reserves the right to search company premises at any time, without warning, to ensure compliance with our policies on employee safety, workplace violence, harassment, theft, drug and alcohol use, and possession of prohibited items. The company may search company property, including but not limited to lockers, desks, file cabinets, storage areas, and work spaces. If you use a lock on any item of company property (a locker or file cabinet, for example), you must give a copy of the key or combination to your immediate supervisor. The company may also search personal property brought onto company premises, including but not limited to toolboxes, briefcases, backpacks, purses, and bags.

TELEPHONE MONITORING

The company reserves the right to monitor calls made from or received on company telephones. Therefore, no employee should expect that conversations made on company telephones will be private.

EMPLOYEE PRIVACY

Here are some alternative clauses regarding property searches and telephone monitoring:

- *Employees do not have a right to privacy in their work spaces or in any other property belonging to the company. The company reserves the right to search company property at any time, without warning, to ensure compliance with our policies on employee safety, workplace violence, harassment, theft, drug and alcohol use, and possession of prohibited items. Company property includes, but is not limited to, lockers, desks, file cabinets, storage areas, and work spaces. If you use a lock on any item of company property (a locker or file cabinet, for example), you must give a copy of the key or combination to (name of person).*

- *The company has designated telephones that employees may use for personal calls. Calls made from these phones will not be monitored. Employees may make personal calls during their breaks; if you must make a personal call during your work hours, you are expected to keep the conversation brief. Telephones for personal calls are located _____.*

COMPUTERS, E-MAIL, INTERNET

E-MAIL

Lane's Garden provides employees with computer equipment, including an Internet connection and access to an electronic communications system, to enable them to perform their jobs successfully. This policy governs your use of the company's e-mail system.

USE OF THE E-MAIL SYSTEM

The e-mail system is intended for official company business. Although you may use the e-mail system for personal messages, you may do so during nonworking hours only. If you send personal messages through the company's e-mail system, you must exercise discretion as to the number and type of messages you send. Any employee who abuses this privilege may be subject to discipline.

E-MAIL IS NOT PRIVATE

E-mail messages sent using company communications equipment are the property of the company. We reserve the right to access, monitor, read, and copy e-mail messages at any time, for any reason. You should not expect that any e-mail message you send using company equipment—including messages you consider to be, or label as, personal—will be private.

Here are some alternative clauses regarding using the e-mail system and e-mail privacy:

- *The e-mail system is to be used for official company business only – not for personal reasons.*

- *E-mail messages sent using company communications equipment are the property of the company. The company's monitoring software automatically creates a copy of every message you draft— even if you never send it. Company personnel will regularly read these copies to make sure that no employee violates this policy. You should not expect that any e-mail message you draft or send using company equipment—including messages you consider to be personal—will be private.*

- *E-mail messages sent using company communications equipment are the property of the company. The company's software automatically searches the messages you send for questionable content—including sexual or racial comments, threats, company trade secrets or competitive information, and inappropriate language. Any message deemed questionable will be forwarded to, and read by, company management. In addition, the company reserves the right to read any message, even if the software does not single it out for review. You should not expect that any e-mail message you send using company equipment—including messages you consider to be personal—will be private.*

COMPUTERS, E-MAIL, INTERNET

E-MAIL RULES

All of our policies and rules of conduct apply to employee use of the e-mail system. This means, for example, that you may not use the e-mail system to send harassing or discriminatory messages, including messages with explicit sexual content or pornographic images; to send threatening messages; or to solicit others to purchase items for non-company purposes.

We expect you to exercise discretion in using electronic communications equipment. When you send e-mail using the company's communications equipment, you are representing the company. Make sure that your messages are professional and appropriate, in tone and content. Remember, although e-mail may seem like a private conversation, e-mail can be printed, saved, and forwarded to unintended recipients. You should not send any e-mail that you would not want your boss, your mother, or our company's competitors to read.

DELETING E-MAILS

Because of the large volume of e-mails our company sends and receives, we discourage employees from storing large numbers of e-mail messages.

Please make a regular practice of deleting e-mails after you have read and responded to them. If you need to save a particular e-mail, you may print out a paper copy, archive the e-mail, or save it on your hard drive or disk. The company will purge e-mail messages that have not been archived after 14 days.

LANE'S GARDEN

FLORAL & GIFTS

VIOLATIONS

Any employee who violates this policy can be subject to discipline, up to and including discharge.

GUIDELINES FOR E-MAIL WRITING

1. Always spell check or proofread. E-mail is official company correspondence. Spelling errors in e-mail are all too common—and they look sloppy and unprofessional. Always take the time to check for spelling errors before you send e-mail.

2. Use lowercase and capital letters in the same way that you would in a letter. Using all capital letters is the e-mail equivalent of shouting at someone—and it can be hard on the eyes. Failing to use capital letters at all (to begin a sentence or a formal noun) can confuse your reader and seem overly cute. Unless you are writing poetry, use standard capitalization.

3. Remember your audience. Although e-mail encourages informal communication, that might not be the most appropriate style to use if you are addressing the CEO of an important customer. Remember that your e-mail can be forwarded to unintended recipients—some of whom may not appreciate joking comments or informalities.

4. Do not use e-mail for confidential matters. Again, remember the unintended recipient—your e-mail might be forwarded to someone you did not anticipate or might be sitting on a printer for all to see. If you need to have a confidential discussion, do it in person or over the phone.

COMPUTERS, E-MAIL, INTERNET

LANE'S GARDEN
FLORAL & GIFTS

5. Send messages sparingly. There is rarely a need to copy everyone in the company on an e-mail. Carefully consider who really needs to see the message and address it accordingly.

6. Always think before you send. Resist the urge to respond in anger, to "flame" your recipient, or to get emotional. Although e-mail gives you the opportunity to respond immediately, you do not have to take it.

INTERNET USE

We may provide you with computer equipment and capabilities, including Internet access, to help you perform your job. This policy governs your use of that equipment to access the Internet.

PERSONAL USE OF THE INTERNET

Our network and Internet access are for official company business only. Employees may access the Internet for personal use only outside of work hours and only in accordance with the other terms of this policy. An employee who engages in excessive Internet use, or who violates any other provision of this policy may be subject to discipline.

Here is an alternative clause regarding personal use of the Internet:

- *Our network and Internet access are for official company business only. Employees may not access the Internet for personal use at any time. Any employee who uses the company's Internet access for personal reasons, or who violates any other provision of this policy, may be subject to discipline.*

COMPUTERS, E-MAIL, INTERNET

PROHIBITED USES
OF THE INTERNET

Employees may not, at any time, access the Internet using company equipment for any of the following purposes:

- To visit Web sites that feature pornography, gambling, or violent images, or are otherwise inappropriate in the workplace.

- To operate an outside business, solicit money for personal purposes, or to otherwise act for personal financial gain—this includes running online auctions.

- To download software, articles, or other printed materials in violation of copyright laws.

- To download any software program without the express consent of (name of person).

- To read, open, or download any file from the Internet without first screening that file for viruses using the company's virus detection software.

INTERNET USE IS NOT PRIVATE

We reserve the right to monitor employee use of the Internet at any time, to ensure compliance with this policy. You should not expect that your use of the Internet—including but not limited to the sites you visit, the amount of time you spend online, and the communications you have—will be private.

Here is an alternative clause regarding Internet privacy:

- *To assure that employees comply with this policy, we use filtering software that will block your access to prohibited sites. However, some inappropriate Web sites may escape detection by the software. The fact that you can access a particular site does not necessarily mean that site is appropriate for workplace viewing. We also use monitoring software to keep track of the sites an employee visits and how much time is spent at a particular site, among other things. You should not expect that your use of the Internet – including but not limited to the sites you visit, the amount of time you spend online, and the communications you have – will be private.*

LANE'S GARDEN

FLORAL & GIFTS

SOFTWARE USE

It is our company's policy to use licensed software only in accordance with the terms of its license agreement. Violating a license agreement is not only unethical—it is illegal and can subject the company to criminal prosecution and substantial monetary penalties. To help us adhere to this policy, employees may not do any of the following without permission from (insert name of person):

- Make a copy of any company software program for any reason.
- Install a company software program on a home computer.
- Install a personal software program (software owned by the employee) on any company computer.
- Download any software program from the Internet to a company computer.

The company may audit company-owned computers at any time to ensure compliance with this policy.

COMPUTERS, E-MAIL, INTERNET

EMPLOYEE RECORDS

YOUR PERSONNEL FILE

Lane's Garden maintains a personnel file on each employee to allow us to make decisions and take actions that are personally relevant to you, including notifying your family in case of an emergency, calculating income tax deductions and withholdings, and paying for appropriate insurance coverage.

Although we cannot list here all of the types of documents that we keep in your personnel file, examples include: your employment application and/or resume and emergency contact form. We do not keep medical records or work eligibility forms in your personnel file. Those are kept separately.

Your personnel file is physically kept by Mary Vandercless. Contact her with any questions.

CONFIDENTIALITY OF PERSONNEL FILES

Because the information in your personnel file is by nature personal, we keep the file as confidential as possible. We allow access to your file only on a need-to-know basis.

PLEASE NOTIFY US IF YOUR INFORMATION CHANGES

Because we use the information in your personnel file to take actions on your behalf, it is important that the information in that file be accurate. Please notify (insert name of person) whenever any of the following changes:

- your name
- your mailing address
- your phone number
- your dependents
- the number of dependents you are designating for income tax withholding
- your marital status
- the name and phone number of the individual whom we should notify in case of an emergency, or restrictions on your driver's license.

EMPLOYEE RECORDS

Inspecting Your Records

Because the text of this policy depends on the specifics of your company and state law, we cannot provide you with a standard policy to use. Please see the main discussion for assistance in drafting this policy language yourself.

WORK ELIGIBILITY RECORDS

In compliance with federal law, all newly hired employees must present proof that they are legally eligible to work in the United States. We must keep records related to that proof, including a copy of the Form I-9 that each employee completes for us.

Those forms are kept as confidential as possible. We do not keep them in your personnel file.

If you would like more information about your I-9 form, contact Mary Vandercless.

MEDICAL RECORDS

We understand the particularly sensitive nature of an employee's medical records, so we do not place any such records in the employee's personnel file. We keep all medical records in a separate and secure place. If you have any questions about the storage of your medical records or about inspecting your medical records, contact Mary Vandercless.

EMPLOYEE RECORDS

POLICY AGAINST ALCOHOL AND ILLEGAL DRUG-USE

Lane's Garden is committed to providing a safe, comfortable, and productive work environment for its employees. We recognize that employees who abuse drugs or alcohol at work, or who appear at work under the influence of illegal drugs or alcohol, harm both themselves and the work environment.

As a result, we prohibit employees from doing the following:

- appearing at work under the influence of alcohol or illegal drugs

- conducting company business while under the influence of alcohol or illegal drugs (even if the employee is not on work premises at the time)

- using alcohol or illegal drugs on the work site

- using alcohol or illegal drugs while conducting company business (even if the employee is not on work premises at the time)

- possessing, buying, selling, or distributing alcohol or illegal drugs on the work site

- possessing, buying, selling, or distributing alcohol or illegal drugs while conducting company business (even if the employee is not on work premises at the time).

Illegal drug use includes more than just outlawed drugs such as marijuana, cocaine, or heroin. It also includes the misuse of otherwise legal prescription and over-the-counter drugs.

DRUGS AND ALCOHOL

DRUGS AND ALCOHOL

This policy covers times when employees are on call but not working and times when employees are driving company vehicles or using company equipment.

Employees who violate this policy may face disciplinary action, up to and including discharge.

INSPECTIONS TO ENFORCE DRUG AND ALCOHOL POLICY

We reserve the right to inspect employees, their possessions, and their work spaces to enforce our policy against illegal drug and alcohol use.

Here are some additional optional clauses for serving alcohol at functions:

- *This policy does not prohibit employees from consuming alcohol while entertaining clients or prospective clients. However, employees may not consume alcohol to the point of intoxication, nor may they consume alcohol if they are going to drive. In addition, employees must always conduct themselves professionally and appropriately while on company business.*

- *We do not prohibit employees from consuming alcohol at social or business functions that we sponsor where alcohol is served. Even at these functions, however, employees may not consume alcohol to the point of intoxication or to the point that they endanger their own safety or the safety of others. In addition, employees involved in security and employees who work with heavy or dangerous machinery or materials may not consume any alcohol at these functions if they will be returning to work that same day.*

Drug Testing

Because the text of this policy depends on the specifics of your company and state law, we cannot provide you with a standard policy to use. Please see the main discussion for assistance in drafting this policy language yourself.

LANE'S GARDEN

FLORAL & GIFTS

LEAVE TO PARTICIPATE IN REHABILITATION PROGRAM

We believe that employees who have a substance abuse problem can help themselves by enrolling in a rehabilitation program. Not only will overcoming their problem help these employees in their personal lives, it will help them to be more effective and productive workers. Although we cannot guarantee that we will grant this leave to all employees who request it, employees who would like to participate in a rehabilitation program may, subject to approval, be able to use up to 4 weeks of unpaid leave from work to attend the program.

Employees will be entitled to health and other benefits while on rehabilitation leave. Employees will not be allowed to accrue vacation and other benefits while on rehabilitation leave.

At the end of the rehabilitation leave, we will require proof that the employee successfully completed the program.

To learn more about this type of leave, including whether you qualify for it, the circumstances under which it is granted, and the requirements that you must meet, contact Mary Vandercless. We will keep all conversations regarding employee substance abuse problems as confidential as possible.

DRUGS AND ALCOHOL

DRUGS AND ALCOHOL

Please note that even as you might be seeking assistance for your substance abuse problem, we still expect you to meet the same standards of performance, productivity, and conduct that we expect of all employees. We reserve the right to discipline you—up to and including discharge—for failing to meet those standards.

Rehabilitation and Your EAP

If you offer an Employee Assistance Program, here is an alternative clause:

- *Because we care about the health and welfare of our employees, your benefits package includes an Employee Assistance Program (EAP) that provides assistance to employees who suffer from substance abuse problems, personal problems, or emotional problems. If you would like such assistance, see Mary Vandercless for information about our EAP program. Your request for assistance will be kept as confidential as possible. Please note that even as you might be seeking assistance for your substance abuse problem, we still expect you to meet the same standards of performance, productivity, and conduct that we expect of all employees. We reserve the right to discipline you for failing to meet those standards.*

TRADE SECRETS/CONFLICTS OF INTEREST

LANE'S GARDEN
FLORAL & GIFTS

CONFIDENTIALITY AND TRADE SECRETS

Keeping our company's trade secrets confidential makes us competitive. During your employment here, you will periodically learn sensitive information, either because you help to develop that information or because you need that information to do your job. It is important for the health of this business—and for the well-being of employees who depend on this business for their livelihood—that you keep information you learn through your employment confidential. Employees who improperly disclose sensitive, confidential information, proprietary information, or trade secret information to anyone outside the company will face disciplinary action, up to and including discharge. After you leave this company, you are still legally prohibited from disclosing sensitive, proprietary, trade secret, or confidential information. If you disclose such information, we will seek legal remedies.

Here is an additional clause for companies with confidentiality procedures in place :

- *Because of the grave importance of keeping certain information confidential, this company follows practices designed to alert employees to sensitive and confidential information, to limit access to that information, and to inform employees about what disclosures are and are not acceptable. We expect employees to follow these procedures. Employees who fail to do so face discipline, up to and including discharge. To find out more about these procedures, refer to _____. If you have any questions about these procedures, contact (name of person).*

LANE'S GARDEN

FLORAL & GIFTS

CONFLICTS OF INTEREST

Our company's success depends on the hard work, dedication, and integrity of everyone who works here. In turn, our employees' livelihood depends on the success of our company.

Because we depend on our employees, and because they depend on us, we expect all employees to devote their energies and loyalties to our company. We do not allow employees to engage in any activities or relationships that create either an actual conflict of interest or the potential for a conflict of interest. Although we cannot list every activity or relationship that would create either an actual or potential conflict of interest, examples of activities that violate this policy include the following:

- working for a competitor or customer or vendor as a part-time employee, full-time employee, consultant, or independent contractor, or in any other capacity

- owning an interest in a competitor, customer, vendor, or anyone else who seeks to do business with this company

- using the resources of this company for personal gain, and

- using your position in this company for personal gain.

Employees who violate this policy face disciplinary action, up to and including discharge. If you are unsure about whether an activity might violate this policy, or if you have any questions at all about this policy, please talk to Mary Vandercless.

(sidebar) TRADE SECRETS/CONFLICTS OF INTEREST

OUR COMMITMENT TO EQUAL EMPLOYMENT OPPORTUNITY

Lane's Garden is strongly committed to providing equal employment opportunity for all employees and all applicants for employment.

For us this is the only acceptable way to do business. All employment decisions at our company—including those relating to hiring, promotion, transfers, benefits, compensation, placement, and discharge—will be made without regard to race, color, religion, sex, or national origin. Any employee or applicant who believes that he or she has been discriminated against in violation of this policy should immediately file a complaint with Mary Vandercless, as explained in our Complaint Policy. We encourage you to come forward if you have suffered or witnessed what you believe to be discrimination—we cannot solve the problem until you let us know about it. The company will not retaliate, or allow retaliation, against any employee or applicant who complains of discrimination, assists in an investigation of possible discrimination, or files an administrative charge or lawsuit alleging discrimination.

Managers are required to report any discriminatory conduct or incidents, as described in our Complaint Policy.

Our company will not tolerate discrimination against any employee or applicant. We will take immediate and appropriate disciplinary action against any employee who violates this policy.

DISCRIMINATION & HARASSMENT

HARASSMENT
WILL NOT BE TOLERATED

It is our policy and our responsibility to provide our employees with a workplace free from harassment. Harassment on the basis of race, color, religion, sex, or national origin undermines our workplace morale and our commitment to treat each other with dignity and respect. Accordingly, harassment will not be tolerated at our company.

Harassment can take many forms, including but not limited to touching or other unwanted physical contact, posting offensive cartoons or pictures, using slurs or other derogatory terms, telling offensive or lewd jokes and stories, and sending e-mail messages with offensive content. Unwanted sexual advances, requests for sexual favors and sexually suggestive gestures, jokes, propositions, e-mail messages, or other communications all constitute harassment.

If you experience or witness any form of harassment in the workplace, please immediately notify the company by following the steps outlined in our Complaint Policy (see Section __ of this handbook). We encourage you to come forward with complaints – the sooner we learn about the problem, the sooner we can take steps to resolve it. The company will not retaliate, or allow retaliation, against anyone who complains of harassment, assists in a harassment investigation, or files an administrative charge or lawsuit alleging harassment. All managers are required to report any incidents of harassment immediately, as set forth in our Complaint Policy.

Complaints will be investigated quickly. Those who are found to have violated this policy will be subject to appropriate disciplinary action, up to and including discharge.

DISCRIMINATION & HARASSMENT

LANE'S GARDEN

FLORAL & GIFTS

COMPLAINT PROCEDURES

Lane's Garden is committed to providing a safe and productive work environment, free of threats to the health, safety, and well-being of our workers. These threats include, but are not limited to, harassment, discrimination, violations of health and safety rules, and violence.

Any employee who witnesses or is subject to inappropriate conduct in the workplace may complain to his or her immediate supervisor or to any company officer. Any supervisor, manager, or company officer who receives a complaint about, hears of, or witnesses any inappropriate conduct is required to notify Mary Vandercless immediately. Inappropriate conduct includes any conduct prohibited by our policies about harassment, discrimination, discipline, workplace violence, health and safety, and drug and alcohol use.

In addition, we encourage employees to come forward with any workplace complaint, even if the subject of the complaint is not explicitly covered by our written policies.

We encourage you to come forward with complaints immediately, so we can take whatever action is needed to handle the problem. After a complaint has been made, Mary Vandercless will determine how to handle it. For serious complaints alleging harassment, discrimination, and other illegal conduct, we will immediately conduct a complete and impartial investigation.

All complaints will be handled as confidentially as possible. When the investigation is complete, the company will take corrective action, if appropriate.

COMPLAINT POLICIES

We will not engage in or allow retaliation against any employee who makes a good faith complaint or participates in an investigation. If you believe that you are being subjected to any kind of negative treatment because you made or were questioned about a complaint, report the conduct immediately to Mary Vandercless.

OUR DOORS ARE OPEN TO YOU

We want to maintain a positive and pleasant environment for all of our employees. To help us meet this goal, Lane's Garden has an open-door policy. Employees are encouraged to report work-related concerns.

If something about your job is bothering you, or if you have a question, concern, suggestion, or problem related to your work, please discuss it with your immediate supervisor as soon as possible. If for any reason you do not feel comfortable bringing the matter to your supervisor, feel free to raise the issue with any company officer. We encourage you to come forward and make your concerns known to the company.

We cannot solve the problem if we do not know about it.

COMPLAINT POLICIES

ENDING EMPLOYMENT

FINAL PAYCHECKS

Final paychecks will include all compensation earned but not paid through the date of discharge.

SEVERANCE PAY

Employees may be eligible for severance pay upon discharge of their employment. Employees must meet all of the following criteria:

- you must have worked for the company for at least one year prior to your discharge
- you must not have resigned, and
- your employment must have been discharged for reasons other than misconduct or violation of company rules.
- Eligible employees will receive 1 week of severance pay for every full year of employment with Lane's Garden.

Here are some alternate policies for severance pay:

- *Our company does not make severance payment to discharged employees, whether they resign, are laid off, or are fired for any reason.*

- *Generally, (insert company name) does not make severance payment to discharged employees, whether they resign, are laid off, or are fired for any reason. However, we reserve the right to pay severance to a discharged employee. Decisions about severance pay will be made on a case-by-case basis and are entirely within the discretion of the company. No employee has a right to severance pay, and you should not expect to receive it.*

ENDING EMPLOYMENT

CONTINUING YOUR HEALTH INSURANCE COVERAGE

Lane's Garden offers employees group health insurance coverage as a benefit of employment. If you are no longer eligible for insurance coverage because of a reduction in hours, because you resigned, or because you are discharged for reasons other than serious misconduct, you have the right to continue your health insurance coverage for up to 6 months. You will have to pay the cost of this coverage.

Others covered by your insurance (your spouse and children, for example) also have the right to continue coverage if they are no longer eligible for certain reasons. If you and your spouse divorce or legally separate, or if you die while in our employ, your spouse may continue coverage under our group health plan. When your children lose their dependent status, they may continue their health care as well. In any of these situations, your family members are entitled to up to 6 months of continued health care. They must pay the cost of this coverage.

You will receive an initial notice of your right to continued health insurance coverage when you first become eligible for health insurance under the company's group plan. You will receive an additional notice when your hours are reduced, you resign, or you are discharged. This second notice will tell you how to choose continuation coverage, what your obligations will be, and the cost of insurance. You must notify us if any of your family members become eligible for continued coverage due to divorce, separation, or reaching the age of majority.

ENDING EMPLOYMENT

EXIT INTERVIEWS

We will hold an exit interview with every departing employee who requests one. We strongly encourage employees to schedule exit interviews. The interview provides the employee the opportunity to relate his or her experience here. We greatly value these comments.

The exit interview also gives us a chance to handle some practical matters relating to the end of your employment. You will be expected to return all company property at the interview. You will also have an opportunity to ask any questions you might have about insurance, benefits, final paychecks, references, or any other matter relating to your employment.

Here is an alternate clause for exit interviews:

- *We will hold an exit interview with every employee who leaves the company for any reason. During the interview, you will have the opportunity to tell us about your employment experience here—what you liked, what you did not like, and where you think we can improve. We greatly value these comments. The exit interview also gives us a chance to handle some practical matters relating to the end of your employment. You will be expected to return all company property at the interview. You will also have an opportunity to ask any questions you might have about insurance, benefits, final paychecks, references, or any other matter relating to your employment.*

ENDING EMPLOYMENT

REFERENCES

When we are contacted by prospective employers seeking information about former employees, we will release the following data only: the positions the employee held, the dates the employee worked for our company, and the employee's salary or rate of pay. If you would like us to give a more detailed reference, you must provide us a written release giving us your permission to respond to a reference request. We will respond only to written reference requests, and we will respond only in writing. Please direct all reference requests to Mary Vandercless.

Here is an alternate clause for references:

- *When we are contacted by prospective employers seeking information about former employees, we will release the following data only: the position(s) the employee held, the dates the employee worked for our company, and the employee's salary or rate of pay.*

FORMS

There are a number of forms that should be included with your employee handbook. Perhaps the most important is the Employee Handbook Acknowledgement. It should be signed by every employee and kept in each person's personnel file.

Employee Handbook Acknowledgement

My signature below acknowledges I have received a copy of the company's employee handbook, and that I understand it is my responsibility to read and understand the information and policies it contains.

I also acknowledge and understand that no part of this handbook constitutes a promise or contract for continued employment. My signature below acknowledges that I understand that my employment with the company is "at will" and that I or my employer can terminate or end the employment relationship at any time and for any reason allowable by law, with or without offering reason and with or without notice or severance compensation of any kind.

I understand that no one can alter the employment relationship through verbal contract and that the only modifications to the employment relationship must be in writing, signed by executive management and the human resources director and myself, and that in absence of any written documentation to the contrary, my employment will continue to be "at will."

I understand and acknowledge that the company has the right, without prior notice, to modify, amend, or terminate policies, practices, benefit plans, and other programs within the limits and requirements imposed by law. The company will make all reasonable efforts to notify employees of any changes to policies or this handbook as soon as possible, via written communication or updates to this handbook.

_____   _____

Employee's Signature   Date

_____   _____

Employee's Name (Print)   Title

Payroll Deduction Authorization Form

I have requested an advance from (insert company name). This advance is a loan that I am fully obligated to repay. In consideration of the company's decision to grant this request, I agree to repay the company through payroll deductions. I hereby authorize the company to withhold $_____ from my paycheck in _____ equal installments to repay the advance. The total amount deducted from my pay shall be equal to the amount of the advance.

If my employment is discharged or I resign before this advance is repaid, I hereby authorize the company to deduct the full amount I still owe the company from my final paycheck, if allowed by law.

_____   _____
Employee's Signature   Date

_____   _____
Employee's Name (Print)   Title

Expense Reimbursement Form

Date of Expense	Item or Service Purchased	Reason for Expense	Cost	Receipt Attached

EMPLOYEE'S SIGNATURE   DATE SUBMITTED

EMPLOYEE'S NAME (PRINT)

SUPERVISOR'S SIGNATURE   DATE APPROVED

SUPERVISOR'S NAME (PRINT)

We are a Drug-Free Employer

At (insert company name), we pride ourselves on a safe work environment. In doing so, it is our belief that we cannot provide employees with safe surroundings if we have an employee who is under the influence of narcotics or other mind-altering drugs. Occasionally without warning we will perform random drug testing. In addition, if an employee appears to be under the influence by exhibiting irrational behavior or slurring of speech, the employee may be asked to undergo a drug screening. Please indicate by signing below that you understand and fully accept the policy as a condition of employment.

_____   _____

EMPLOYEE'S SIGNATURE   DATE SUBMITTED

_____

EMPLOYEE'S NAME (PRINT)

_____   _____

SUPERVISOR'S SIGNATURE   DATE APPROVED

_____

SUPERVISOR'S NAME (PRINT)

Section Two

WRITING THE MOM AND POP MANUAL FOR SMALL BUSINESS

As an added benefit of purchasing this manual, we have added in a short sample section for mom and pop businesses or small business owners. These businesses may have as few as one or two employees or could have several. Either way, they view themselves as small and so do the employees who work for them. In the community they are thought of as a small business as well. However, mom and pop businesses still need a guide to follow.

Keep in mind, as a small business; you can keep the mechanics of an employee-handbook down to a minimum. After all, the employees are probably not expecting a manual to follow so they will be surprised to see you are organized and meticulous enough to have one. In the following last pages, you will see a sample you can follow in setting up your mom and pop handbook.

INTRODUCTION AND COMPANY STATEMENT

Introduction

Meriam Price started this deli in 1990. She saw a need for fast, friendly service in a deli and decided it was time to give customers what they wanted and deserved—a cheap meal in the cleanest environment. Meriam's Deli has built a clientele based on those principles since the beginning, and customers have enjoyed many family times at Meriam's Deli.

Here at Meriam's Deli, folks come in for the food and service. We make sure they get the best of both. We have served more than 500,000 sandwiches since our humble beginnings and we hope to serve another 500,000. We think it is an achievable goal because we know our repeat customers will continue to come in as long as we provide fast service and great food.

In a mom and pop's handbook, there is no reason to go into a lengthy spiel about the company. Think brief. Everything in a small business is smaller and more laid-back. The manual is no different. Your employees will be needed on the floor taking care of customers so keep your employee handbook simple!

SECTION TWO: NATURE OF EMPLOYMENT

Welcome to Meriam's Deli.
We Hope You Will Feel at Home Here

We do not make any guarantees of employment beyond your current shift. We have been in business since 1990 and have no plans of closing in the near future but we make our statement known as to the nature of employment.

Employment with Meriam's Deli is "at will," meaning that you can resign at any time, and we can let you go at any time. We can terminate your employment with or without reason, and you can resign with or without reason. Notices are not required by either party.

Understand, when employment is considered "at will," we make no promises to you as our employee and expect none from you as our employee regarding the length of employment.

HIRING AND EMPLOYMENT

EOE

Meriam's Deli is an equal opportunity employer (EOE). Because we are an EOE, we follow all laws pertaining to fair and equal employment. We do not discriminate against employees or customers and expect the same from our employees.

Hiring and Recruiting Measures

We believe it takes someone committed to excellence to work at Meriam's Deli. We value our employees, and most of them begin to work with us based on past relationships with us as a customer. We welcome your suggestions for employment, and we are always on the lookout for someone who is a Meriam Deli fit. We listen to our employees and hire from within based on recommendations. While we prefer not to hire spouses, we will look at each opportunity on a case-by-case basis.

NEW EMPLOYEE INFORMATION

Training for the New Employee

Even if you have worked in the food industry before, we believe it is crucial to train you specifically for working at Meriam's Deli for efficiency and safety. Within a couple of days, you will be trained appropriately. There is a training period as discussed in 4:2. Understand, there are no dumb questions. If you have a question, we want you to ask. If you need help with any of the equipment or you do not understand something, please always ask. It is crucial to your success at Meriam's Deli.

Training Period

Even though we train our employees quickly, you are considered in training for the first 90 days of your employment with Meriam's Deli. During this time, look to your peers and your managers to help you learn the recipes, the menu, pricing and handling of equipment. Learn from those who have been with Meriam's for some time. The training period is an excellent time to prove you are right for the job and for the managers to get to know you. This is the time when we, as the employer and you, as the employee, can decide if we are well matched for the employer-employee arrangement.

When you begin your training period, you will meet (Name of person) who will explain our benefits. He will also discuss payroll with you. You will then be assigned to work with Meriam during the training period. She will introduce you to work at the deli. She will work with you hands-on to let you know what she expects and generally help you to get acquainted with the way we do things at Meriam's Deli.

We want to hear your questions and suggestions. We are always on the lookout for bright employees who can offer us a better way to do things.

After the 90-day training period, employees will meet with Dan Price again to discuss vacation time such as sick leave and PTO time. Again, we hire employees who work based on "free will" and with the understanding either party can terminate the relationship at any time.

Proof of Eligibility

All employees must complete an I-9 form that confirms identity and eligibility to work in the United States. This is a federal law and is non-negotiable. See (name of person) for information or if you have questions. No employee will be allowed on the cook line or at the counter without completing this process.

REFERENCES

Delpo, Amy and Guerin, Lisa; *Create Your Own Handbook A Legal and Practical Guide*, 2005 Nolo

Accentuate Services
www.accentuateservices.com

United States Department of Labor (**http://www.dol.gov/**)
   Occupational Health and Safety Administration
   Bureau of Labor Statistics
   Employment Standards Administration
   Employment and Training Administration
   Employee Benefits Security Administration

Miscrosoft.com template designs (**www.microsoft.com**)

US Equal Employment Opportunity Commission (EEOC)
   http://www.eeoc.gov/

GLOSSARY

360 Degree Feedback A method in which an employee may receive feedback on their own performance from their supervisor and up to eight co-workers, reporting staff members, or customers.

A

Absence or Absent (Scheduled) A period of time off from work that is previously planned during a normally scheduled work period.

Absence or Absent (Unscheduled) A period of time off from work during a normally scheduled work period that has not been planned.

Absenteeism Policy A policy that provides guidance within an organization regarding managing an employee's chronic absence from work.

Active Employee Employee in pay status.

ADA Americans with Disabilities Act. The ADA defines disability as a physical or mental impairment that substantially limits one or more of the major life activities; anyone having a record of such an impairment; or anyone regarded as having such an impairment.

Adaptive Cultures The environment within a company where employees, who are innovative, are encouraged, and initiative is awarded by middle and lower-level managers.

Affirmative Action (AA) An effort by an employer to correct past discrimination and prevent current and future discrimination within the workplace.

Age Discrimination in Employment Act (ADEA) of 1967 A law prohibiting discrimination against workers 40 and over in any employment decision. It applies to most employers with 20 or more employees.

Agile Organization An organization that is able to adapt quickly to changing circumstances and customer demands.

Annuitant A former employee or beneficiary entitled to an annuity under a retirement system established for employees.

Attendance Policy The expectations and guidelines for employees to report to work as written, distributed, and enforced by an organization.

B

Background Checking or Background Investigation The act of looking into a person's employment, security or financial history before offering employment or granting a license.

Balanced Scorecard Model The way in which a manager assesses an employee's organizational skills by considering both financial and performance measurements for efficiency, quality, innovation, and responsiveness to customers.

Basic Factors of Production Items having to do with producing deliverables, such as land, labor, capital, and raw materials.

Behavioral Interview An analysis of answers to situational questions that attempts to determine if you have the behavioral characteristics that have been selected as necessary for success in a particular job.

Benefits Additions to employees' base salary, such as health insurance, dental insurance, life insurance, disability insurance, a severance package, or tuition assistance.

Bereavement Policy The portion of an employment contract that provides for a certain amount of time off from work when an employee's spouse or close family member passes away.

Bonus Plan A system of rewards that generally recognizes the performance of a company's key individuals, according to a specified measure of performance.

Bottom-Up Change A gradual process in which the top management in a company consults with several levels of managers in the organization and develops a detailed plan for change with a timetable of events and stages the company will go through.

C

Cafeteria Plan Flexible benefit plans are authorized by Internal Revenue Code Section 125, under which employees may choose from among two or more benefits offered by an employer. Employee deductions to fund the benefits are exempt from federal income tax, FICA, and, in some states, state income tax, withholding. Benefits under a cafeteria plan may include accident and health insurance, dependent care assistance, group legal services, group term life insurance and additional vacation days.

Carrier An entity that offers a health benefits plan.

Check Disposition A code that indicates how an employee's net pay is distributed to the employee, such as via direct deposit.

Clarity of Expectations The concept that before, during, and after strategic decisions are made, managers should have a clear understanding of what is expected of them, as well as an idea of any new rules or strategies.

Coaching A method used by managers and supervisors for providing constructive feedback to employees to help them continue to perform well, or to identify ways in which they can improve their performance.

Cognitive Biases Errors in the methods human decision makers use to process information and reach decisions.

Commission System A system of rewards in which employees are paid based on how much they sell.

Company Infrastructure A work environment in which all activities take place, including the organizational structure, control systems, and culture.

Conflict Aftermath The long-term effects that emerge in the last stage of the conflict process.

Conflict of Interest Situations in which an individual has competing financial, professional, or personal obligations or interests that interfere with his or her ability to perform required duties fairly and objectively.

Congruence The state in which a company's strategy, structure, and controls work together.

Consolidated Omnibus Reconciliation Act (COBRA) of 1985 If an employee terminates employment with the company, he or she may continue to participate in the company's group health plan for a prescribed period of time, usually 18 months.

Coordination of Benefits Coverage by more than one insurance carrier for the same health care expenses. One pays its benefits in full as the primary payer and others pays a reduced benefit as a secondary or third payer. When the primary payer does not cover a particular service and the secondary payer does, the secondary payer will pay up to its benefit limit as if it were the primary payer.

Copay A percentage of the charges for which the employee is responsible when receiving covered services.

Core Competencies Skills, knowledge, and abilities employees must have to perform job functions that are essential to business operations.

Corporate Governance The strategies used to watch over managers and ensure that the actions they take are consistent with the interests of primary stakeholders.

Corporate Social Responsibility The obligation of a company to build certain

social criteria into their strategic decision-making.

Counseling The act of providing daily feedback to employees regarding areas in which their work performance can improve.

Cross Training Developing a multi skilled work force by training employees in the skills necessary to perform various job functions in a business.

Cycle An iteration of the planning process which begins with the corporate mission statement and major corporate goals.

D

Decentralization An organizational hierarchy in which authority has been delegated to divisions, functions, managers, and workers at lower levels in the company.

Defined Benefit Plan A retirement plan that pays participants a fixed periodic benefit or a lump-sum amount, according to a specific formula. It is not an individual account plan.

Demotion A reassignment to a position with a lower pay grade, skill requirement, or level of responsibility than the employee's current position.

Developmental Counseling Supervisors and subordinates identify strengths and weaknesses, resolve performance-related problems, define, and create an appropriate action plan.

Devil's Advocacy A way of improving decision-making by generating a plan and a critical analysis of that plan.

Dialectic Inquiry A way to improve decision-making by generating a plan and a counter-plan.

Differentiation The method a company uses to allocate people and resources to certain tasks in the organization to create value.

Direct Deposit An employee's net pay automatically transmitted into the employee's bank account on or around payday.

Discharge Termination of an employee.

Disciplinary Action Applying corrective action to employees who do not abide by the organization's written performance standards, policies, or rules.

Discipline A process of dealing

with job-related behavior that does not meet communicated performance expectations.

Discrimination Any unfair disadvantage to either an individual or group of individuals who are considered part of a protected class.

Disparate Impact Under the Equal Employment Opportunity (EEO) law, a less favorable effect for one group than for another, usually applying to women and minority groups.

Documentation Written notices, records, forms, memos, and letters used by both sides during disciplinary proceedings.

Downsizing The process of reducing the employees head count in an organization.

Dress Code for Business Casual A company's objective to enable employees to project a professional, business-like image while experiencing the advantages of more casual and relaxed clothing.

E

Early Return to Work Program Programs designed to help employees who have been out of work because of injury or illness to return to work sooner by providing them with less strenuous alternative jobs during recuperation

EEO Equal Employment Opportunity.

Effective Date The date an employee's health coverage begins.

Efficiency The measurement derived from dividing output by input.

EH&S Environmental Health & Safety.

Emotional Intelligence A term that describes a bundle of psychological characteristics that many strong leaders exhibit (self-awareness, self-regulation, motivation, empathy, and social skills).

Empathy The psychological characteristic that refers to understanding the feelings and viewpoints of subordinates and taking them into account when making decisions.

Employee Empowerment The process of enabling or authorizing an individual to think, behave, take action, and control work and decision-making autonomously.

Employee Handbook A document designed to familiarize

employees with matters affecting the employment relationship.

Employee Involvement The act of creating an environment in which people may impact decisions or actions that affect their jobs.

Employee Relations Activities related to developing, maintaining and improving employee relationships by communicating with employees and processing grievances/disputes.

Employee Retention Organizational policies and practices designed to encourage employees to remain employed.

Employee Retirement Income Security Act (ERISA) of 1974 A federal law that established administration of private employee benefit plans, including health care, profit sharing, and pension plans.

Employee Stock Option Plan (ESOP) A system of rewarding employees in which they may buy shares in the company at below-market prices.

Employment-at-Will A legal document that states that an employment relationship may be terminated by the employer or employee at any time without giving a reason.

Employment Eligibility Verification (I-9) The form required by the Department of Homeland Security U.S. Citizenship and Immigration Services to document an employee's eligibility to be employed in America.

Empowerment Relinquishing to an employee the responsibility, control, and decision-making authority over the work he or she performs.

Engagement The process of involving individuals in active decision-making by asking them for their input and by allowing them to refute the merits of one another's ideas and assumptions.

Enrollee The individual in whose name the health plan enrollment is carried.

Equal Pay Act of 1963 A federal law prohibiting employers from discriminating male or female employees in terms of pay when they are performing jobs of comparable worth.

Ergonomics A science of fitting work or workplace to the human body to help avoid injury or illness due to occupational stressors.

Exempt Employee Employees who are not confined by the laws governing standard minimum wage and overtime.

Exit Interview At the time of an employee's resignation, it is used to identify the underlying factors behind an employee's decision to leave.

Explanation The idea that all those who are involved and/or affected should be told the basic reasoning for strategic decisions and why some ideas and inputs may have been overridden.

External Stakeholders All individuals and/or groups outside the internal stakeholders who have a claim on the company.

F

Fair Labor Standards Act (FLSA) The legislation that requires a company to pay a non-exempt employee who works more than a 40 hour week 150 percent of their regular hourly rate for the overtime hours.

Family and Medical Leave Act (FMLA) The legislation which states that covered companies must grant an eligible employee up to 12 weeks of unpaid leave during any 12-month period of time for one or more of the covered reasons.

Federal Insurance Contributions Act (FICA) Taxes imposed under this law fund social security.

Fee-for-Service Plan A traditional type of insurance that allows an eligible employee to use any doctor or hospital. It usually requires payment of a deductible and co-insurance. These plans help control costs by managing some aspects of patient care.

Feedback The information given to or received from another person regarding the impact of their actions on a person, situation, or activity.

FEHA Fair Employment and Housing Act.

Felt Conflict The type of conflict occurring at the stage in which managers start to personalize the disagreement.

Fiscal Year An accounting period of 12 months.

Fitness for Duty A "doctor's note" used by the employer to determine a candidate's ability to perform the functions of a job following illness or injury.

Flat Structure An organization with few hierarchical levels resulting in a relatively wide span of control.

Flexible Benefit Plan A benefit program offering employees a choice between permissible taxable benefits and nontaxable benefits such as life and health insurance, vacations, retirement plans, and child/dependent care. The employee may determine benefits dollars are allocated. It is regulated under IRC 125.

Flexible Scheduling Non-traditional schedules provided to employees for greater flexibility in meeting their personal needs.

FLSA Fair Labor Standards Act, a Federal law, which establishes certain minimum requirements for employees' hours of work, wages, premium overtime, and payroll records.

FMLA Family Medical Leave Act.

Focus Group A small group of individuals who brainstorm about a particular topic.

Fringe Benefit Any benefit above one's pay.

Functional Boss The one who holds primary responsibility for a function.

Functional Orientation A state in which functions evolve and grow more remote from one another, in turn causing each function to develop a different view of the strategic issues facing the company.

Functional Structure An organizational method of grouping people based on their common expertise and experience or on the same set of resources those people use.

G

Garnishment A court action initiated by a creditor to obtain a part of an employee's earnings before they are turned over to the employee.

General Manager A person who bears all responsibility for the organization's overall performance or that of one of its major self-contained divisions.

Generation X The generation of people who were born between 1965 and 1976 (or 1980, depending on the source). "Gen Xers," as they have been called, tend to be independent, informal, entrepreneurial, and seek emotional maturity.

Goal The future state a company attempts to reach.

Goal Characteristics The attributes of a meaningful goal: precise and measurable, meeting

of important issues, challenging but realistic, and time period-specific.

Green Card A legal card issued to an alien granting him or her the right to work legally in and to become a citizen of the United States.

Grievance A formal complaint by an employee or group of employees seeking remedy for unfair treatment or violation of a union contract.

Gross Pay Wages, before necessary taxes and voluntary deductions have been withheld.

Group-Based Bonus System A type of reward system in which project teams are rewarded based on group productivity.

Groupthink A method of decision-making in which a group of decision-makers embarks on a course of action without questioning potentially hidden assumptions.

H

Head Count Refers to the average number of employees (not contractors) who work full-time and part-time.

Health Benefits Plan A group

insurance policy or contract, medical or hospital service agreement, membership or subscription contract, or similar group arrangement provided by a carrier for the purpose of providing, paying for, or reimbursing expenses for health services.

Health Insurance Portability and Accountability Act (HIPAA) of 1996 The purpose of the act was to make health insurance portable from one employer to another to reduce or eliminate the new employer's preexisting condition requirements. The law also includes special enrollment rights and privacy rights and protections.

Health Maintenance Organization (HMO) A health benefits type that provides care through a network of doctors and hospitals in particular geographic or service areas. An employee's eligibility to enroll in an HMO is determined by home address usually.

Health Savings Accounts (HSA) Employees use a tax-free account to pay for qualified medical expenses. Money in the account earns interest and can be used now and in the future. To qualify for a Health Savings Account, an employee must have a High Deductible Health Plan (HDHP), no other health insurance, not be eligible for Medicare, and not be claimed as a dependent on someone else's tax return.

Hidden Disabilities Disabling maladies with symptoms that are not visible.

Horizontal Differentiation The way in which the company focuses on the grouping of people and tasks into functions and divisions to meet the objectives of the business.

Hostile Environment Harassment Discriminatory conduct that is pervasive enough to create a hostile, abusive, or intimidating work environment for a reasonable person.

Human Resources (1) The people who are part of an organization and its operations. (2) The business function that deals with the employees of a company.

I

I-9 *See*: Employment Eligibility Verification.

Independent Contractor A person or a business that performs services or supplies a product for a person or a business under a written or implied contract.

Incentive pay plan A plan providing additional compensation intended to serve as an incentive for excellent performance, exceeding productivity goals or standards, as well as other contributions in accordance with prescribed goals or standards.

Incumbent The current employee filling specific position.

Intermittent/Reduced Schedule Leave Under the Family Medical Leave Act an intermittent and reduced schedule leave is taken in increments of days or hours, alternating with a work schedule.

Internal Governance The way in which the top executives in a company manage individuals within the organization.

Internal Stakeholders Anyone in a company who is affected by that company, whether they are a stockholder or an employee of any level.

Ivory Tower Planning A strategy that treats planning as an exclusive function of top-level management.

J

Job Classification Defining the specific tasks comprising a job so that a description of the duties and responsibilities can be compiled in a job descriptions, usually identified by job codes.

Job Offer Letter A written document that confirms the details of an offer of employment, including details such as the job description, reporting relationship, salary, bonus potential, and benefits.

Job Posting The method of advertising internally for personnel to fill open jobs.

Job-Relatedness An employer must be able to prove that a particular action, policy, or job requirement is related to the actual job.

L

Labor Management Glossary A comprehensive list of the definitions of labor management terms provided by the U.S. Office of Personnel Management.

Latent Conflict The possible conflict that may flare up when the right sort of conditions occur.

Learning Effects The cost savings that come from learning while performing the task.

Legitimate Power The authority a manager holds due to being placed in a formal position in the organization's hierarchy.

M

Mail-Order Drug Program A prescription drug service which fills prescriptions through the mail.

Major Goals Plans that define what the business hopes to meet in the medium- to long-term future.

Management Buyout (MBO) The act of selling a business unit to its management.

Management by Objectives (MBO) A process in which managers participate in their evaluation of their capability to achieve certain organizational goals or performance standards and to meet the given operating budget.

Matrix in the Mind A network of information that allows a company to take global advantage of the skills and abilities of its personnel.

Medicare Managed Care Plan A managed care plan such as an HMO that contracts with Medicare to enroll Medicare beneficiaries. An enrollee must go to the plan's network of doctors and hospitals to receive full benefits and will usually be required to pay a monthly premium and co-payments.

Millennials Current employees who were born between 1980 and 2000. The stereotypical millennial has developed work tendencies from doting parents, a structured life, and more contact with diverse people.

Minimum Wage The minimum amount of compensation per hour for covered, nonexempt employees as defined by the Fair Labor Standards Act (FLSA) and by local states.

Mission Statement A brief but precise definition of what an organization does and why.

Motivation A psychological portion of emotional intelligence that refers to a passion for work that goes beyond money or status and enables a person to pursue goals with energy and persistence.

Multidivisional Structure A type of organizational structure in which each distinct product line or business unit is made to be self-contained, and the corporate headquarters staff monitors unit activities and exercises financial control over each of the divisions.

N

Negativity The concept and expression of unhappiness, anger, or frustration to other employees in the workplace.

Net Pay Income after necessary deductions and taxes have been withheld.

Networking The act of building interpersonal relationships that could be mutually beneficial.

New Employee Orientation Also called Induction. The process of orienting a new employee, usually performed by one or more representatives from the Human Resources department.

Non-Exempt Employee Employees who are protected by the laws governing standard wages and overtime.

O

Operating Budget A plan stating how managers intend to use organizational funds and resources to achieve organizational goals in the most efficient way possible.

Operating Responsibility The authority held by divisional management in a multi-divisional structure to oversee the day-to-day operations.

Operations Manager An individual who is responsible for particular business operations.

Option A level of benefits. Some health benefits plans provide a high (better benefits) and a standard (lower benefits) option. Some provide only one option.

Organization Bonus System A system of rewards based on the performance measurement of the organization during the most recent time period.

Organizational Culture The particular collection of values and norms shared by people in a company which controls the way they interact with each other and with outside stakeholders.

Organizational Norms The expectations that prescribe the appropriate behavior for employees in certain situations.

Organizational Politics The strategies that managers use to obtain and use power to influence business processes to further their own interests.

Organizational Socialization The method of people internalizing and learning the behavior and values of a culture to fit in.

Organizational Values Concept regarding the goals that individuals within an organization should pursue and what behavioral standards they should follow to achieve these goals.

Orientation *See*: New Employee Orientation.

Out-of-Pocket Maximum (OPM) The maximum amount an employee must pay for eligible health expenses each year before the health plan begins paying 100 percent of subsequent eligible expenses in that year.

Output Control A system in which certain managers estimate appropriate goals for each division, department and employee, and measure actual performance in relation to these goals.

Outsourcing The act of paying another individual or business to perform certain internal processes or functions.

OWCP The Office of Workers Compensation Programs, U.S. Department of Labor.

P

Pay Grade A designated pay range within a salary structure.

Perceived Conflict Conflict that occurs when managers are made aware of clashes within an organization.

Performance Management A policy for dealing with behavior on the job that does not meet expected and communicated performance standards.

Piecework Plan A system of rewards in which output can be more accurately measured, and employees are paid based on a set amount for each unit of produced output.

Power The capability of an individual, function, or division to cause another to do something it would not have done if left to its own devices.

Price Cutting The act of reducing the price of products or services below a standard level in an attempt to reduce competition and lead to increased sales.

Primary Payer Under coordinated benefits where there are two health benefit carriers, the primary payer pays benefits first and to the extent of its coverage.

Product-Team Structure A type of organization in which people are assigned to permanent teams that perform cross-functional tasks.

Profit Ratios A way of measuring

how efficiently a company uses its resources.

Profit-Sharing System A system of rewards that compensates employees based on the company's profit during a specified time period.

Progressive Discipline A process for dealing with behavior on the job which does not meet expected and communicated performance standards.

Project Boss The figure of authority for a particular project.

Project Management The process of applying knowledge, skills, tools, and techniques to a wide range of activities in order to meet the requirements of the particular project.

Promotion The act of advancing an employee to a position with a higher salary range maximum.

R

Recognition A practice of providing attention or favorable notice to another person.

Recruiter People who are hired by a company to find and qualify new employees for the organization.

Re-engineering The basic rethinking and major redesign of business processes to realize dramatic improvements in important, current performance in areas such as cost, quality, service, and speed.

Representativeness An error in decision-making in which decision-makers try to make generalizations from a smaller sample or a single clear anecdote.

Restructuring A method of improving company performance by reducing the level of differentiation and downsizing the number of employees to decrease operating expenses.

Return on Investment (ROI) A measurement of the money that has been gained as a result of certain resource investments.

Rule of Three A requirement that selection of new employee must be made from the highest three eligible candidates who are available for the job for which they applied.

S

Salary Range The range of salaries that is assigned to each grade level.

Salary Structure Series of grade

levels and related salary ranges.

Secondary Payer Under coordinating benefits, the health plan that pays benefits after the primary payer has paid its full benefits.

Self-Awareness The psychological characteristic of a person's emotional intelligence in which he is able to understand his own moods, emotions, drives, and his effect on others.

Self-Discipline The psychological ability to control one's own behavior.

Self-Regulation The psychological ability to control or redirect one's own disruptive impulses or moods.

Service The business activity that concentrates on providing after-sales service and support.

Sexual Harassment The act of an employee's making continued, unwelcome sexual advances, requests for sexual favors, and/or other verbal or physical conduct of a sexual nature toward another employee against her or his wishes.

Sexual Harassment Investigation The process of looking into an employee's complaint of sexual or other harassment in the workplace. *See:* Sexual Harassment.

Simple Structure A type of organization generally used by small entrepreneurial companies that produce a small number of related products for a specific market segment, and one person usually takes on the bulk of the managerial tasks.

Social Skills The psychological ability to interact purposefully with others at a friendly level.

Span of Control The number of employees a manager manages directly.

Standardization The level at which a business defines how decisions are to be made so that the behavior of employees becomes predictable.

Strategic Control The process in which managers monitor an organization's ongoing activities, members, and correct performance as necessary.

Strategic Leadership The charisma of someone that enables him to articulate a strategic vision for the company or part of the company and motivates others to share that vision.

Strategic Responsibility The task of corporate headquarters staff to oversee long-term plans and provide the guidance for inter-divisional projects.

Strategy The actions a company takes to achieve one or more of its goals or superior performance.

Strategy Formulation The analysis of an organization's external and internal environment resulting in the selection of an appropriate strategy.

Strategy Implementation The act of putting into place an organization's chosen strategy.

Survivor Annuitant A surviving family member of a deceased employee or retiree who is entitled to an annuity under a retirement system established for employees.

T

Tall Structure An organization that has several hierarchical levels resulting in a relatively narrow span of control.

Tips An employee who receives cash tips of twenty dollars ($20) or more in a month must report them to his employer by the 10th day of the following month. Employers are subject to FICA taxes on the reported tip income.

Top-Down Change An adjustment that occurs when a strong upper-management team analyzes how to alter strategy and structure, recommends an appropriate course of action, and moves quickly to restructure and implement change in the organization.

Total Quality Management (TQM) A philosophy of management that concentrates on improving the quality of a company's products and services and stresses that all operations should head toward this goal.

Trust—Interpersonal and Organizational The condition in which a person or business is ready to interact with someone or something without walls or hesitation.

U

Unemployment Compensation A policy created by the Social Security Act of 1935 to protect workers who lost their jobs due to circumstances outside of their own control.

V

Value Statements Statements regarding how the organization will value customers, suppliers, and the internal community, and describing actions which are the living enactment of the fundamental values held by most individuals within the organization.

Values Traits or characteristics that are considered to be worthwhile and that represent an individual's priorities and driving forces.

Vertical Differentiation The method of defining the reporting relationships that link people, tasks, and functions at all levels.

Vision Also called a Mission. A statement of the goals that the company would like to achieve over the medium- to long-term.

W

Withholding Amount(s) deducted from an employee's pay, annuity, or compensation for your share of the cost of health benefits.

Workers' Compensation Pay under subchapter I of chapter 81 of title 5, United States Code, which is payable because of an on-the-job injury or disease. An injury, disease, or medical condition must meet the test of both "arising out of employment" and occurring during the "course of employment" to be covered under the Workers Compensation law.

INDEX